# THE HORNED GOD

Cernunnos
Contemporary carved figure by Bel Bucca

# THE HORNED GOD

FEMINISM AND MEN AS WOUNDING AND
HEALING

JOHN ROWAN

ROUTLEDGE & KEGAN PAUL
LONDON AND NEW YORK

First published in 1987
Reprinted in 1987 by
Routledge & Kegan Paul Ltd
11 New Fetter Lane, London EC4P 4EE

Published in the USA by
Routledge & Kegan Paul Inc.
in association with Methuen Inc.
29 West 35th Street, New York, NY 10001

Set in 11/13 Sabon
and printed in Great Britain
by Butler & Tanner Ltd, Frome, Somerset

Library of Congress Cataloging in Publication Data

Rowan, John.

The horned God

Bibliography: p.
Includes index.
1. Feminism. 2. Masculinity (Psychology)
3. Men—Psychology. Sex role. I. Title.
HQ1154.R766 1987 305.3 86–13887

British Library CIP Data also available

ISBN 0–7102–0674–7

This book is dedicated to
Neil and Sue

# Contents

# *Introduction*

In writing this book I felt great trepidation. For a man to write about feminism is problematic. It's like a white man's book on racism, or an Ulsterman's account of the Irish problem.

In trying to be aware of these issues, I resolved to do at least two things which would make the task possible. One was to write about men rather than about women. Men are my constituency, so to speak, in a way that women are not. I can speak to men about men more legitimately than I can talk to women about men or men about women. So this book is written by a man for other men. Women have much better books than this to read, written by women for women. I have read many of them, over the shoulders of women, as it were. In the same way, I suppose women can read this book if they want to, over the shoulder of a man. But it is not intended to enlighten or entertain women – it is intended to help in starting to fill various enormous gaps in the education of men.

The other thing I tried to do was to make it clear where I was coming from. One of the things we have all learned from feminist writing is that it is not OK to leave out the author. We are less interested now in whether a statement is true – in some totally abstract and pristine sense – and more interested in the place from which the statement is made, the ground on which the person is standing who makes the statement. So in this book I have tried to say what was going on for me in my life at the time when I made certain discoveries or faced certain problems, and the way in which the discovery or problem came to me.

So this book is the record of a journey. It starts in a dark and difficult place, goes through another dark and difficult place, and ends up in a third dark and difficult place. But the first place is full of pain, the second place is a mixture of pain and pleasure, and the third place is more joy than anything else – a hard and bitter sort of joy, it is true, but joy none the less.

What I discovered during the course of writing this book was that virtually all the things people say about men are true, but they don't have to mean what they are usually supposed to mean. For example, men don't often like to be called Male Chauvinist Pigs. But I had a dream in which my passport had a photograph of a boar in place of my own photo. When I went into this with the help of the understanding engendered by this book, I discovered that some of the ancient tribes in what is now Germany worshipped the mother of the gods, and wore as a religious symbol the device of a wild boar. The Germanic boar-god became the doomsday-averting Saviour and Lord of Death. Accordingly the boar was sacrificed at the turn of the year, at Yule, with an apple in his mouth as a resurrection charm. 'Myths of dying gods like Tammuz, Attis and Adonis featured the boar, or boarskin-clad priest' (Walker, 1983). Coming closer to home, the boar was the sacred animal, more than any other, of the Celts. Above all, pigs were believed to come from the Otherworld, and to be guides to the Otherworld. In Britain, Merlin had a pig as a familiar. So the boar, masculine with feminine moon-tusks, has many connections with the Horned God, the Lord of the Animals, we shall meet later in this book. It is therefore very meaningful that the photograph in my passport should be that of a boar. The message is that in some sense I am a boar. And since in this book I am saying that to be male is OK, and the whole book is addressed to men, and is for men, it could be said that I am in myself a true Male Chauvinist Pig. The only difference is that I am in the service of the Goddess. And that makes all the difference, as we shall see in the later chapters of this book.

I would like to thank the men who read earlier drafts of

chapters from this work in progress and made detailed comments, though I have not adopted all of their suggestions and they should not be expected to support anything said here. They are Keith Mothersson, Daniel Cohen and Paul Morrison. I would also like to thank Batya Podos for a great deal of practical help and encouragement.

John Rowan
London
1986

# CHAPTER 1

# *The wound*

I am a man.

At first that may sound like an ordinary sort of a statement, pretty obvious really. So what else is new?

Yet in a way it is a confession, an admission – it is rather as if I were to say – 'Yes, I dropped the bomb on Hiroshima.' Except that it goes further, into the tiny details of everyday life. It is like adding – 'And I'm putting a little arsenic into my wife's tea every day.'

The days when I was discovering this were some of the worst days of my life. My wife had discovered feminism, as I had in theory too, and got busy to confront me on all the things she had been suppressing or not noticing or glossing over for eighteen years of our marriage. As a good revolutionary, I agreed in theory with everything she said: it was important to learn this stuff. But I was being wounded: it hurt. And as a good member of the growth movement, I allowed it to hurt.

This book is all about what I and other men did and are doing to heal that wound, or similar wounds. It is about how I and other men are affected by feminism, and what can be done about it. And I am going to argue that it is important for men to allow themselves to be wounded. The wound is necessary before any healing can happen.

Now obviously there are many different strands within feminism, and one could argue indefinitely about exactly who and what and how and when and where and whither, but what I can't help feeling is at the heart of it is the most basic and straightforward version of radical feminism, which says that the male as such is suspect.

It is men who dominate, it is men who aggress, it is men who run things, it is men who ride roughshod over feelings and subtleties, it is men who run the media of mass communication, it is men who go in for linear thinking and terrible simplification, it is men who set up and maintain the basic hierarchy which goes up in the way shown in Figure 1.

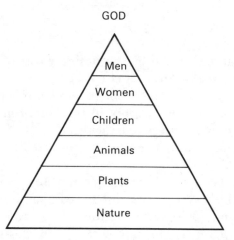

*Figure 1  The world-map of patriarchy. (After Elizabeth Dodson Gray,* Patriarchy as a Conceptual Trap, *Wellesley, Mass.: Roundtable Press, 1982)*

Now this system is often called patriarchy, but it is well to pause for a moment here and see whether this is really the best word to use.

## Patriarchy

This is a term which came into currency in the early 1970s, though it had been used before. It seemed that we had to have a word which spoke of the whole system with all its levels, and 'patriarchy' did just that. It connected the political with the personal, it spoke of the conscious and the unconscious, it included the material and the spiritual, and it emphasised that the language with which we criticised patriarchy was itself patriarchal. The peace campaigner Donna Warnock says this: 'Patriarchy is a society which worships the masculine identity, granting power and privilege to those who reflect and respect the socially-determined masculine sex role' (Warnock, 1982). What is interesting, in fact, is the way in which people concerned with peace and ecology have found the word not only useful but inescapable. It fits very naturally into their argument:

> When the intellect and the dominating, controlling, aggressive tendencies within each individual are defined as the most valuable parts of their being, and those same attributes are emphasised in the political and economic arena, the result is a society characterised by violence, exploitation, a reverence for the scientific as absolute, and a systematic 'rape' of nature for man's enjoyment. The result is patriarchy. (Swain and Koen, 1980)

What is so clear to emerge from this analysis is that feminism, by its opposition to patriarchy, makes patriarchy's boundaries clearer, its shape more well defined, its contrasts more stark:

> The power of patriarchy is such that to see through it requires a special kind of vision, a consciousness of the most 'ordinary' experience. To understand it requires 'thinking across boundaries', as Mary Daly says. To overcome it demands the reinvention of revolution. This consciousness, this vision, this experience, this understanding, this revolutionary politic is feminism. (Warnock, 1982)

This is the language of paradox, because it is only thinking across boundaries which can establish new boundaries, which in turn need to be surpassed, since there is no single day of evolution after which everything is different and forever fine.

The work of rethinking and of revision always needs to continue. Women were the first to see this so well, but now men are having something to say, too:

> Patriarchy, which links characteristics (gentleness, aggressiveness, etc.) to gender, shapes sexuality in such a way as to maintain male power. The masculine game draws strength from homophobia and resorts habitually to violence in its battles on the field of sexual politics. It provides psychological support for the military state and is in its turn stimulated by it. (Kokopeli and Lakey, 1982)

The links are tightly drawn between sexuality and war in this way. The fear of homosexuality and the fear of the female are closely linked to the fear of softness and being a wimp. But weak males are not wimps any more than all strong males are macho, as we shall see later.

Now one of the dangers of the word patriarchy is that it seems to suggest to some people that all that is female is wholly good, and all that is male is totally evil. But this would be a very unpolitical or even counter-revolutionary position. Betsy Wright says in a marvellous essay:

> Reducing social change into a struggle between good and evil and saying that oneself and one's movement belong entirely on the good side is simplistic and similar to the objectification that has hurt women so much.... Social forces are seen *in motion*, not fixed.... Of course, the institution of patriarchy has been terribly cruel and destructive, but it is not a monolith, and understanding its internal dynamics will help enable its opponents to topple its institutions and replace them with something better. (Wright, 1982)

So patriarchy is seen as an historical structure, which came into being and can go out of being, and has internal dynamics which are changing it all the time. It is nothing to do with biological determinism, as some critics suggest. It is about socially and historically defined gender, not about biological sex.

Dworkin (1974) points out that since there are six things involved in sex identity (genetic sex, hormonal sex, gonadal sex, internal sex, external sex, and psychosexual development) and since there can be contradictions of various kinds between any of these, we seem to be 'a multi-sexed species which has its sexuality spread along a vast fluid continuum where the elements called male and female are not discrete.' It is precisely the fault of patriarchy that it takes this amazingly subtle and sensitive mixture and clamps on it two firm and fixed categories, one of which, and one only, is OK. It would be an absurd error for anyone to accept this twofold categorisation and say simply – 'No, it's the other one which is OK'!

It was feminism which allowed us to see that all the struggles against oppression are one struggle, the same struggle, the struggle with patriarchy. It is very important that the black struggle and the gay struggle are one with the women's struggle. A black member of the National Black Feminist Organization once said –

> We are often asked the ugly question, 'Where are your loyalties? To the Black movement or the feminist movement?' Well, it would be nice if we were oppressed as women Monday through Thursday, then oppressed as Blacks the rest of the week. We could combat one or the other on those days – but we have to fight both every day of the week. (Quoted in Dunayevskaya, 1981)

It is feminists who have seen that the ending of patriarchy is not about just one question, the question of equality, of equal rights. It is a full-blooded and two-pronged question which affects everything:

> first, the totality and the depth of the necessary uprooting of this exploitative, sexist, racist society. Second, the dual rhythm of revolution: not just the overthrow of the old, but the creation of the new; not just the reorganization of objective, material foundations but the release of subjective

personal freedom, creativity and talents. In a word, there must be such appreciation of the movement from below, from practice, that we never again let theory and practice get separated. That is the cornerstone. (Dunayevskaya, 1981)

So patriarchy is essentially a unifying term, which enables us to see the single pattern underlying many apparently separate struggles. And we shall see later how important is Gray's (1982) point that 'The decisive question is always, "Who controls the myth system?" – who is in charge of the social and religious construction of reality?'

Now all this is very abstract in a way. It was necessary to put it in because the basic case is very rarely spelt out so succinctly, and I did not want just to refer the reader to other sources. But the real question is – how do men react to this news? How can men respond to this news? And the best way I know of dealing with that is to say how I reacted, and how I responded, together with the men I knew.

I was very split. In one way I was totally convinced and in favour. My wife had been very modest and withdrawn and family-oriented, and now she was going out to three meetings a week, tending bookstalls, helping to organise events, coming back with excited reports about visits to schools and so on – it was obviously very good for her. I read the literature and found it very persuasive, as if saying very obvious things which had been suppressed for a long time and desperately needed saying.

But at an action level I was quite different. I simply held on to my old habits and my own ways in the home as I had always done. And I got confronted on this, day by day. I got accused of rigidity, of not changing, or not really wanting to change.

It seemed to me at the time that my wife was exaggerating. Things couldn't be that bad or that important. She was blowing things up beyond what was reasonable. It was hard to put into words the experience of what all this felt like. I was very struck by a recent piece of Vic Seidler (1985) which does seem to capture the flavour very well.

> I can hear the cry of anger and frustration as if it is directed at me. It is all too familiar, even though I pretend to understand it intellectually, I am always surprised and shocked when this happens. I recognise that something is terribly wrong but I don't really know what to do about it. I'm shaken by the fury and the bitterness. I find it hard to accept that things can be that bad, though I know at some level that they are. Part of me just wants to flee or withdraw. It is as if all long-term heterosexual relationships in our time are doomed. For all my efforts at a more equal relationship I have to recognise how blind and insensitive I am. It is harder to know what to do about it.

That is just how I felt at the time. It was a sort of baffled feeling – 'How on earth am I ever going to get it right?' I would really intend to listen to what my wife said, but find myself criticising her logic, her motives, her sense of balance – anything to avoid really listening or hearing what she was really trying to say.

One thing I got very clearly from all this, though, was a clear vision that women are dominated and oppressed in ways that men are not dominated or oppressed. It is true that there are some groups of men who from time to time do get treated badly – gay men, disabled men, handicapped men and so on – but even these get treated better by society than the equivalent groups of women. It is as if there were a gradient or slope in society, such that men can move easily, aided by gravity, as it were, while women have to move up the hill and against the grain.

This I could see quite well, but whenever I said this to another man, he would deny it and resist it. He would always claim to be oppressed, sometimes even claiming to be oppressed by women. The best answer I found was in Karen Lindsay's statement: 'The error here is the failure to recognise that such men are not, in fact, oppressed by the patriarchy – some of their patriarchal privilege is withheld because they are not top-notch oppressors' (Lindsay, 1979). Some men I respect still do not agree with this statement, but it seems to me that unless it is fully accepted, we have still not got the point – that there is a radical rift in society, whereby men are given supremacy and women are continually relegated to service roles.

In a patriarchy male ways of talking, thinking and acting are generally held to be better than female ways of talking, thinking and acting. Men are rewarded more, therefore, in all kinds of ways, but financially in particular.

Again men don't like to hear this, and object that many female ways are highly rewarded – look at the success of women novelists and romance writers, look at the success of actresses like Elizabeth Taylor. Such men need to look at the massive evidence accumulated, for example, in Judy Chicago's art work (and the books based on it) *The Dinner Party*. In this work, the artist and her hundreds of collaborators have examined women's history, and come up with over a thousand great women, eminent in many fields, who were finally killed, forgotten or otherwise squashed by a patriarchal society which could not admit that they existed. Their names should be in every history book, but they are missing because they are women. This is the social story.

The sexual story is even worse. The history of *suttee* in India, of footbinding in China, of genital mutilation in Africa, of witch-hunts in Europe, of gynaecology in the USA, have been documented by Mary Daly (1979). The war against women celebrated in pornography has been documented by Laura Lederer (1980) and her collaborators. The importance of rape as a process of intimidation which has very widespread effects on women is documented by Andrea Dworkin (1974). And a more recent approach to much of this material is to be found in Rhodes and McNeill (1985).

It is one thing to read these things in books; it is quite another to have someone in your own home facing you with such issues day by day. It was clear that I was oppressing my wife, and I didn't know what to do about it. But I was learning all the time, painfully and with difficulty. I learned about patriarchal values.

## Patriarchal values

Values under patriarchy are basically supremacy values, but are hardly ever talked about or referred to in those terms. The basic assumption is that all things must be divided into superior and inferior, and general supremacy given to that which is superior. This is a method of control, and it is thought to be the only method of control which is stable and natural. If it is not clear at any point who or what is superior, a competition or contest will reveal the truth. Thus the basic way of deciding things under patriarchy is by a power struggle. Physical coercion is there all the time under patriarchy, sometimes overt and sometimes covert. Violence is normal and natural, where it proves to be necessary.

These values enter into everything – work, leisure, politics, religion, even sex. 'Fucking' means both intercourse and exploitation or assault. Rape is the end logic of male sexuality under patriarchy.

Again, men object to this assertion. We think of our needs for love and affection and warmth, as expressed, for example, in Hite (1981). We think that men are rather tame – not many rapists in our circle of acquaintances. But any serious study that looks beneath the surface very quickly finds the male need to dominate and be in control. Even in the Hite report there are a lot of indications of this. And in psychoanalytic studies by Seidenberg (1973) and other deep studies such as Fasteau (1975) and Adcock (1982) it comes out very clearly. The reason why men resist so strongly the truth of the assertion is because to admit it would be to admit the whole patriarchal case in a very personal way which comes very close. Men are quite content to discuss patriarchy at a general level, where it affects whole societies, but when it comes to the personal, it hurts too much.

This can easily be seen in the home. In the home we can see

domination and submission in action. If a man and a woman are living together in a shared home, and particularly if they are married, and even more particularly if there are children, the household tasks will move, due to the pressures of a patriarchal culture, in such a way that the most boring tasks are carried out by the women. For the evidence of this, see Oakley (1974). When this is pointed out to men on the spot, they come back with lines such as:

> You're so much better at ironing than I am.
> I'm not really cut out for that. I *hate* it more than you do.
> Of course I'll do it! (And then we don't.)
> Why should I have to do it to your standards?
> Housework is so trivial!

All the lines which are dealt with so well by Pat Mainardi in Morgan (1970) are relevant here. What is going on is an unspoken mini-oppression. This was all so familiar to me personally. I had used every one of those lines when talking to my wife, and to see them written down in a book was shocking and hurtful. Although it was right, and just, and even funny as written, it pained me. I felt really wounded and beaten-up.

But I knew that I had to persevere. What I was doing reflected the domination-submission culture in which I had been brought up, and which I had maintained even while denouncing it. This is just the sort of contradiction which Lucia Sanchez Saornil referred to when she said:

> You, can you imagine a bourgeois saying that the workers
> should be emancipated? So, if you find it logical that, like
> the bourgeois with the worker, the anarchist as a man keeps
> woman chained up, it is absurd to hear him shout 'women
> must be emancipated'. And if he does shout it, how can one
> not say to him 'you start'. (Quoted in Reynaud, 1983)

It is in this atmosphere that rape comes to seem almost normal. Every study of rapists which has been carried out (e.g. Groth,

1979) finds that rapists are quite normal, not particularly different from other men. It is power they want much more than sex.

Pornography reinforces this culture too, no matter how soft
or innocuous it may seem to be, because it shows women
basically in service to the phallus. They are there for the benefit
of the phallus, which rises up to salute them. As long as they
play along with the phallus, they are acceptable and interesting;
the moment they do not, they are objectionable. As long as they
flatter the phallus, they can stay; as soon as they do not, they
must go. Their worth is conditional.

This is one of the main areas where men deceive themselves.
They consider to be freedom and liberation what is actually
serfdom and slavery. Women are encouraged to be free only in
the way that suits and serves the phallus. This is because there
is a curious idealisation of the phallus in many men, quite
unconscious and unremarked. There is a sort of insane phallic
optimism, which assumes that women really want sex just in
exactly the way that feeds the phallus – only they are too
inhibited to say so, or to own up to it even in private. In reality,
women are much more variable in their sexual needs and wishes
than the phallus has time for. See the many examples of this in
Hite (1976).

But of course the phallus is not to be taken for granted either.
As soon as we come to any serious questioning of the phallus,
we find, as Litewka in Snodgrass (1977) says, that it is highly
socialised – in other words, it is taught to be that way by
messages coming in from the culture ever since childhood. We
are taught as men that women are 'other' – they are like some
complicated subject (or object) that has to be studied, learned,
mastered. We are taught by other males that it is OK to be
fixated on parts of the female, particularly the breasts:

And in movies, on TV, in advertisements, where else can we
look when the camera's eye focuses on breasts? So our eye
is trained and we fixate. Emotionally, too. We learn that if
we do that, we will eventually get pleasure and have fun.
And be men. Be seen as male. Be reacted to as male. (Litewka)

This leads to the third characteristic of the phallic approach –
conquest. Reynaud (1983) points out that this is so important
because for so many men sex is not actually pleasurable, due to
their inability to let go and experience the pleasure. If we say
that orgasm is precisely this letting go, this surrender to the
involuntary movements of the whole body, then ejaculation is
not orgasm, and many men are nonorgasmic. So power becomes
the main thing. It is often more satisfying to a man to get a
woman's knickers off than actually to have sex with her. The
one gives immediate power gratification, while the other makes
extra demands too. And so, as Litewka points out, male sexual
responses often have little or nothing to do with the specific
female who is present. The socialised phallus is interested in
ejaculation, not in being friends.

But when it comes to the crunch, even the phallus is only a
servant in the need for control, power and domination. This
need for domination is so strong in our culture that it extends
right up and down the hierarchy (see Figure 1). But men deny
this. We do not feel as if we are dominating. We are usually not
sophisticated in the way that, for example, Su Negrin (1972) is.
Here are some brief examples of what she says:

*What being dominated feels like*
Being dominated feels like always wondering if I did the right
    thing.
Being dominated feels like worrying how I look when
    someone's coming over.
Being dominated feels like singing along instead of singing.
Being dominated feels like being depressed and not knowing
    why.
Being dominated feels like needing someone instead of loving
    her.
Being dominated feels like realizing that all the men I ever
    lived with can't spell and have lousy handwriting and that
    I can do both well.
Being dominated feels like being good at school instead of
    finding out what I wanted to know.

Being dominated feels like not being able to distinguish myself from my kids.

Being dominated feels like believing it when my (male) lover told me I was as possessive as a sponge.

*What dominating feels like*

Dominating feels like wondering if my son, Paul, lies to me and if so why.

Dominating feels like sleeping with my younger sister's boyfriend without giving it a thought.

Dominating feels like hearing a new Cuban rock album and feeling good about the revolution because it produced music I really liked, and not even realizing I liked it because it sounded like American music.

Dominating feels like needing directions and mindlessly bypassing a Chinese man to search for someone else.

Dominating feels like throwing away Paul's toys without asking him.

Dominating feels like *not knowing* how much of my compulsive behaviour those two kids have internalized.

Dominating feels like realizing I've lost touch with my own centre.

We as men have very often lost touch with our own centres. It is only because I was lucky enough to find mine again that I could even begin to write this book. Only then could I see for myself what was going on, and what I was implicated in. What I am implicated in is nothing much less than a war of men against women.

But it is not the old sex war, which is the subject of so many films, cartoons, stories and poems. It is a new feminist challenge.

The old sex war is something we are all familiar with. The conversation goes something like this:

First man: You know, women really are oppressed in this system – it has to change.

Second man: I don't know, men have a pretty rough time

too – at least women don't have to go out and fight if there's a war.

And so the argument goes on. We have slipped from a discussion of feminism to the argy-bargy of the old sex war in two sentences. In the old sex war there is a kind of evenly matched symmetry – it goes something like this.

| THE MEN SAY | THE WOMEN SAY |
|---|---|
| Women are oversensitive | Men are insensitive |
| Women are martyrs | Men are selfish |
| Women are too picky about sex | Men are obsessed with sex |
| All women want out of a relationship is children | All men want out of a relationship is sex |
| Women are too dainty and houseproud | Men are too messy, dirty and careless |
| Women are too timid | Men are too aggressive |
| Women are only interested in children and clothes | Men are only interested in sport and cars |
| Women just want to gossip together | Men just want to go down to the pub with their mates |
| Women are too devious | Men are too brash |
| Women have it easy – they don't have to go to war or down the mine | Men have it easy – they don't have to do all the shit work |
| Women are like children | Men are like children |
| Women are unfair | Men are unfair |
| Women want to be flattered | Men want their egos massaged |

This is really all quite comfortable for men, because we always have a ready riposte and can keep our end up in an argument. But the thing about the new feminist challenge is that it is not symmetrical. There is no equivalent charge to hurl back. If women get 65% of the wage of a man for doing the same work, if women are kept out of the high-ranking jobs, if women are only tolerated in service roles (or up on pedestals), if women can only be accepted if they play the male game in the male way, there is no answer except to say 'You're the oppressed one – it's up to you to change it.' But that is offensive if it actually means that the man is going to feed and reinforce the patriarchal system which keeps things that way.

But if men do begin to feel that things need to be changed, there are two crucial questions we have to answer. How can we change? and what do we change into?

There are subsidiary questions, too, such as – What is our motivation to change? Are we just trying to help the women, or is there something in it for us too?

All these questions, and others like them, have been addressed by the anti-sexist men's movement, and so it will be profitable to turn now to a consideration of this response to the challenge of feminism.

But I can't leave this chapter without remembering the worst wound of all, the one that sticks in my mind still now, ten years later, when my wife said that she had heard a theory that originally there were women on the earth, and that men had come from another planet. They were really aliens, not human beings at all. And she looked at me and said she could believe this theory. That was the worst thing she ever said to me, and I can still feel the pain of that moment.

The trouble with men is that they read something like that and think to themselves – 'Can't he see she is full of shit? What rubbish!' When they would do better to think about the depth of feeling that must have been behind her, to say something like that. And it is that depth of feeling which needs to be dealt with, not the accuracy of the statement itself. If she feels that deeply, if she is that alienated, if the gap seems so great, there must be something very wrong, something that desperately cries out to be healed.

# CHAPTER 2

# First channel of healing

I was driven nearly crazy by all this stuff. At the time when it really started, I had just started working at home as a freelance market researcher, and my desk and chair had taken over half the bedroom in our flat, because there was nowhere else to put them. So I was actually encroaching more on my wife, both in terms of space and in terms of the time I was at home, than ever before. She was at home all day, our children being 18, 17, 12 and 9 at the time. I was rushing all over the country doing interviews and group discussions, spending a lot of time in political meetings and demonstrations, attending AHP committee meetings, going to growth groups at weekends, giving lectures on social psychology, going to conferences, helping to organise events like the first Fritz Perls workshop in England, writing poetry and going to poetry meetings, helping to launch a new radical psychology magazine and a few other things.

I wanted my wife to explain to me in words of one syllable what exactly I had to do to be acceptable to feminists. I did try to see her point, but I also kept on resisting it too. Eventually she got me to go to a men's group to sort it all out.

Around 1970 the first anti-patriarchal men's groups were meeting in the United States, and in 1971 the first magazine with this orientation, called *Brother*, was published in San Francisco. About a year later the first groups started in Britain.

## Men's groups

These groups consisted mainly of men who had been told by their friends or wives in the women's liberation movement that they should go and work things out with other men. They could be uncomfortable places.

When I went to my first men's group, in London in 1972, it was trying to decide what to call itself. Should it be Men Against Sexism, Men's Liberation or Unbecoming Men? (All these had been used by men's groups in America.) Although it was a little frustrating to be spending so much time arguing about a name, these different titles actually represented different strains within the movement, which separated out more and more as time went by.

Men Against Sexism was the heaviest title, much favoured by politicos who saw the whole thing as much like other political struggles. The tendency was to link the whole thing with Marxist thinking. The slogan which emerged from this was −'No women's liberation without revolution: No revolution without women's liberation.' There were often close links with socialist feminism.

Men's Liberation was a rather more complex outlook, which eventually split into a number of other strands, but essentially it found itself wanting to explore male consciousness for its own sake. What was it like to be male? What was it like to be with other men, with no agenda and no task to perform? What was it like to be warm and affectionate with other men without getting into homosexual panic?

Unbecoming Men was an attempt to relate directly to the radical feminists – the strongest and most militant wing of the women's liberation movement. It involved a radical questioning of everything to do with masculinity, and a determination not to flinch even from effeminacy, if that's what it took to deal with the problem. Unfortunately the radical feminists were never very impressed with any of these groups, then or now.

Of course, I am making it much too stark. Things at the time were by no means so simple. Some socialists, for example, saw

Men Against Sexism as being much closer to radical feminism than I have suggested here. In any case the distinctions were never as marked or definite here in Britain as they were in the United States.

The men's group I first went to was very strong on theory. We all knew the theory of feminism as it had emerged up to that point. We had read our Friedan and our Greer, our de Beauvoir and our Firestone, our Maccoby and our Bem, our Figes and our Hacker, our Koedt and our Millett, our Mitchell and our Morgan, our Roszak and our Weissstein. We were enthusiastic about the theory; I had myself just written a chapter on sex differences for a book on social psychology.

But of course all this theory was written by women, from a woman's standpoint, with women's interests in mind. It was challenging rather than helpful. We felt stimulated rather than satisfied. And the way the group had started did not help. Basically it had come from women – in my case my wife – saying to us something like this:

> It is our belief that if men want to raise their own
> consciousnesses, then they should form their own groups and
> organize themselves – women have been trying for centuries
> to educate men to the need for a more equal society and are
> always having to put their energy into men's needs and
> wants. . . . If the men . . . are so keen on being educated then
> they should do some thinking themselves instead of sponging
> off women's output and strength . . . [They should] do
> something on their own, using their own time and energy.
> (Reply to a letter in women's centre newsletter, 1985)

This is of course a perfectly legitimate message, but it makes for an uneasy start. It means that in such a men's group there is a feeling of absent women peering over one's shoulder. And these absent women knowing more, feeling it more, sensing more, intuiting more, of what the whole thing was about. As if we were there to catch up.

Again some men I have shown this to object that I am being

too hard here, and feel that there were some more positive things going on too. Certainly many men did discover a lot of warm, open, close and brotherly feelings towards other men which they had never been aware of before. I myself made one very good friend, who helped me a lot to face the challenges of feminism in a way that was supportive and unafraid.

In June 1973 there was a Men Against Sexism conference in London. It was pretty small and rather intellectual, having been organised mainly by politicos. But it was a start in bringing together the scattered groups and getting more of a feeling of being some kind of a movement. It led to the production of a magazine called *Brothers*, which contained a powerful and intense article by Keith Paton called 'Crisis and Renewal', later reprinted in *Self and Society*. Keith was from an early date one of the most insightful and articulate men in the movement, pushing himself further and further all the time into the forbidden and painful areas which most people avoided.

For example, in this early publication Keith was talking already about 'the 60/40 game'. This is where a man living with a feminist admits that she is most often right about feminist issues, particularly when she confronts him on his own actions. He allows as how she has more insight, more feeling, more motive in such things. But in his head this gets translated into a kind of proportion or percentage. She can't be right all the time – no one can be right all the time. So maybe she's right 90 per cent of the time, or 80 per cent, or 70 per cent, or 60 per cent. Of course, this means that every issue still has to be argued and fought out, because this might be one of the – admittedly minority – cases where he is right.

> And all the other cases the same (funnily enough) so you don't give an inch. The 60/40 game is a heap of *shit*. You know it but you won't *break*. You insist on fragmenting your POWER, your BLOODYMINDEDNESS, into a hundred little issues – on each of which (once safely parcelled out) *you* are prepared to argue rationally, it's just that she gets so worked up. (Paton, 1974)

This rings as true today as it did then. And this is the sort of issue which kept on emerging in the men's groups. No wonder they were uncomfortable places to be, and no wonder that they kept on breaking down into small groups of shaken men huddling together for warmth.

In October 1973 a second issue of the magazine came out, this time under the title *Men Against Sexism*, and it seemed clear that more groups were forming and the movement growing. In November, a men's conference was held in Birmingham, and was again encouraging and productive. April 1974 saw a Leeds conference on men against sexism, and about the same time came out the third and very interesting issue of the magazine, this time under the title *Brothers Against Sexism*.

It was in 1974 that two contradictory things happened, one positive and the other negative, which were to have profound consequences for the still young network of men's groups.

The positive one was that the growth movement started to get closer to the women's liberation movement. In January 1974 the Association for Humanistic Psychology ran a one-day workshop on sexual energy and gender identity, which I co-led with Maureen Forrester, using techniques I had picked up from Ed Elkin and others. (Again the USA was ahead of us in these matters: in February 1973 there had been an article for men in *Ms.* magazine by Warren Farrell, entitled 'Guidelines for consciousness-raising'.) In May there was a ground-breaking meeting put on by Quaesitor (the biggest growth centre in Europe at the time) aimed at bringing together therapy and politics. It took place at the Collegiate Theatre in London, and about 350 people attended. It was addressed by Jerry Rubin, who at that time was still political, and also very much interested in gestalt therapy; Stella Resnick, a gestalt therapist very close to him; Rick Carlson, a radical lawyer; Denny Yuson, who at that time was a group leader specialising in Synanon-influenced encounter marathons; and Brian Dempsey, a young group leader working with disadvantaged youth.

Some very moving speeches were made, both from the platform and the floor, and one of these latter, by Vic Seidler, a lecturer at Goldsmiths' College, suggested that a group be formed to meet regularly on questions of therapy and politics. This did in fact happen, and a motley assortment of people started meeting, at first calling themselves the Radical Therapy Group. Over a period of some months this group got smaller, tougher and more sure of what it was doing, and by the following year was known as Red Therapy. It focussed on functioning as a leaderless therapy group for people involved in political struggles, although it was also interested in creating a political critique of the whole area of therapy, personal growth, counselling and the like. The biggest single contingent consisted of members of a small party based in Liverpool and called Big Flame, which later threw them out for being too interested in sexual politics and personal issues.

Over the years 1974–7 Red Therapy flourished and eventually produced a fat pamphlet about what we had discovered. Later still, two of the women in the group published a book (Ernst and Goodison, 1981) in which many of the lessons were spelled out. When the group broke up, some of the women joined the Women's Therapy Centre, and some of the men (including Vic Seidler) started the magazine *Achilles Heel* for anti-sexist men. One of the key ideas that emerged from this group was that of 'unconsciousness raising', and we shall come back to that in the next chapter.

Some changes had been taking place in my own life. Things had become so uncomfortable for me at home in 1972 that in January 1973 I moved out and went to live in a little shared flat in Crouch End. In April, however, I broke my hip, and went back to my wife. We then decided to build a hut in the garden, to house my desk and chair, my books and papers and so on. This we did, and this hut, complete with telephone, heater and a growing collection of pinned-up postcards and posters, became the main working centre of my life for the next five years. This reduced the pressure on my wife's space, and also cut down on the incidental meetings between us, so that the situation became less tense, and less intense.

At this time, as well as my other activities, I was taking a course at the Polytechnic of North London under John South-gate, and taking my first steps as an organisation development consultant. I was, of course, an almost totally absent father to my children, but at the time I had little or no insight into this. My wife was a very good mother, with a lot of care and devotion to the children, and she had the support of her mother and father (who lived downstairs) to take care of the children if she wanted to go out in the evenings. It later seemed very sad (as it certainly does now) that I missed their childhood so much, that I took so little interest in them. At the time, I was enjoying myself so much that it didn't seem to matter. But let's go back to the story.

All through 1974 the men's movement was growing, and five issues of a news sheet were produced in London, giving details of new groups being formed. A lively leaflet was produced by the men's group I was in at the time, and we gave this out at the Windsor Free Festival that year. It felt as though real head-way was being made. But then in November disaster struck.

Up until that time, the groups had all been quite clearly heterosexual in orientation, because of the kind of origins I have been outlining. Gay men were very much in a minority, some groups having one and other groups none. On the whole, gay men tended to be far ahead of straight men in their under-standing of patriarchy, because of feeling some of the raw lash of patriarchal prejudice themselves. In a men's group, they tended to have little to learn and much to teach.

But in the big conference in London in November 1974, a group of gay men made their presence felt very powerfully. They complained of homophobic prejudice and lack of understanding in the conference itself, and denounced the straight men for being shifty and hypocritical about their position. They exposed all the most embarrassing features of the men's movement, along the lines of the following indictment, taken from an anonymous article in *Brothers Against Sexism*:

> Straight men derive privileges from being straight men as
> such. To be straight is to *continue* to derive those privileges

irrespective of what one wills.... You are trying to make heterosexual relations work. Why? For the sake of 'your women'? I doubt it. Surely for yourselves *because you don't want to make it with men*.... Of course men won't turn you on if you don't *try* – you'll never make the transition in the abstract: you have to meet them, get close to them, start touching them, kiss each other hello and goodbye; it may take you weeks to get an erection with a man.... But do you want to try? We fancy what is good for our egos; we're turned on by the ego boost, off by the threat. You may *like* other men but you wouldn't depend on them for emotional support ... *you like what women have to offer*, which is the direct expression of their oppression; focus upon your ego-needs.... You claim to want to struggle against your own sexism and yet you refuse to make *central* and *primary* and *before everything else*, the task of breaking with *gender-roles*. You want to stop being men, but without stopping being men.... If men can learn to relate to each other equally, really equally, then the problem of relating to women will be half solved; we'd be ready to relate to them properly (the other half is their responsibility). If, on the other hand, you are not prepared to abolish your gender role, then you are merely playing – devising more and more subtle ways of 'treating your women right' – they're still *women*, they're still *yours* – and you're still *men*.... ADMIT TO YOURSELVES that gay men make you freak and run for reassurance to your women and to your own particular world of straight men. Admit that you freak and then we, together, can deal with it.... There are a thousand ways to deceive yourself. But in the end the only way forward is to *really* open yourself up to the mirror image of yourself and experience through another, *yourself as a man* (you are a male remember) – and build something from the ruins of your male ego that will result.

Reading this is one thing – easy to avoid its message in any one of a hundred ways – but being faced by a group of men confronting you with it on the spot is different and much more scary. I have quoted it at length because the experience of this conference virtually shattered the men's movement for three years. The guilt was just too much to bear.

True, there was a sexuality conference in Brighton in January 1975, and a big meeting in London in the same month. And in February of that year the most ambitious workshop yet put on by the growth movement took place, with straight men, straight women, gay men and gay women all in the same group, and four facilitators, of whom I was one. But in Spring 1975 the last issue of the magazine came out, under the title *The Pig's Last Grunt*, expressing the complete demoralisation which most of us felt.

There were some men who kept the flame alight, however. A group of men started the East London Men's Centre in Redman Road, and began to write material which later became the basis for the magazine *Achilles Heel*. These men, some of whom were in the Red Therapy group already mentioned, did not lose heart and hung on and kept the faith, so to speak.

Of course it is possible to think up all sorts of good answers to the position put forward by the gay men, but the discomfort remains. It was even made worse by some of the women, who pointed out that gay men were still often very masculine:

> Masculinity is not just heterosexuality. It is power-seeking, it is being closed-up, competitive, drab, insensitive, interested in things and goals rather than people and processes. Most male homosexuals are 90% masculine in their general behaviour. (Anonymous)

So if being straight is being oppressive, and being gay is still being oppressive, what place is there for a man at all? Some men at this time took this all the way. John Stoltenberg wrote an essay in 1974, reprinted in Snodgrass (1977), entitled 'Refusing to be a man', in which he referred to himself as not heterosexual, not homosexual and not bisexual:

I intend to live as a moral androgyne. I am genitally male, but I endeavour with my heart to rid my life of male sexual behaviour programming.

Some men went further down this line and wrote 'The Effeminist Manifesto' (again in Snodgrass, 1977) in which they said that their purpose was to change themselves from non-masculinists to anti-masculinists, using effeminism as the means.

But even this was not acceptable to the feminists they were supposed to be supporting. As two of them said (also in Snodgrass, 1977):

As you yourself point out, 'all men are the enemies' (and one of us, Karla, was one of the Redstockings who formulated that theory), so in the end you are as much of an enemy as the rest. All the male privileges you so eagerly give up are immediately handed back to you by the male power structure. (Jay and Rook)

No wonder that the men's movement crumbled, when the reception by women of even its most heroic and extreme efforts was as negative as this.

So instead of the continued growth of men's groups, what now happened was an increasing integration of sexual politics with ordinary political activity. This particularly happened in Big Flame and IMG, but also in various libertarian groups not affiliated to any one organisation. Some of the IMG men brought out a pamphlet called *Sexism, Sexuality and Class Struggle* midway through 1975. It said things like this:

It is glaringly obvious how great a reactionary force sexism is both within the revolutionary class and within revolutionary organizations. We cannot afford to willingly hold back the development of revolutionary class consciousness because we are not prepared to challenge the motor force of sexism within ourselves.

This was fine, a good extension of awareness of the problem, but it offered no new solutions.

One of the most interesting attempts to link sexual politics with ordinary politics came from a new organisation called Alternative Socialism, which had a close link with the long established magazine *Peace News*, and produced a pamphlet mainly written by Keith Paton. There was a big meeting in York in 1975, and two big meetings in August 1976, one in London and one at Lauriston Hall. A newsletter was started about that time.

Alternative Socialism had the basic idea of putting together three things – the struggle against patriarchy, the struggle against capitalism and the new thinking on ecology and alternative technologies. It introduced new concepts such as Malemployment, and pointed out that no matter how many people were unemployed, far more people were malemployed – working on projects which are not socially beneficial. But most of all it emphasised the *centrality* of the struggle against patriarchy. It pointed out that:

> All of us have been deeply damaged by sexism in different ways, men even more so in some ways since they still imagine they are superior and that they stand to lose from respecting women's autonomy, learning from them and re-owning the repressed sides of our personalities. . . . Men need to own and come to terms with all sorts of irrational fears and hatreds against gay people, women and their bodies, menstruation, etc.

Alternative Socialism had more insight into patriarchy than any political grouping before or since. But it was fatally flawed by being a mixed movement led by men. Even though Keith Paton, who later changed his name to Motherson, was far ahead of most men in his own anti-patriarchal development, he was still a man. And this produced tensions which led to the destruction of Alternative Socialism within quite a short period. Some of the Alternative Socialism women wrote an important pamphlet called *Is it Worthwhile Working in a Mixed Group?* (Long and Coghill, 1977) to which the answer was basically *No*. One ray of hope was held out – that in a mixed group working on patriarchal issues both the men and the women need their own separate single-sex support group. Then it may work. But of course this is quite hard to arrange.

Another reason for the demise of Alternative Socialism may have been the fact that, like many similar groups, it had a lot of hangups and reservations about any kind of structure or planning. This made it impossible to arrive at any very strong identity or centre. I am not sure about this: it seems to me now that the time was not right for it, because the narrowness and negativity of the 1970s was already drawing in. In any case, the problems of Alternative Socialism are not quite the same as the problems of men's groups.

There is a curious difference between a men's group and a women's group in this context. I have done a lot of investigation of this, and have found consistently that women's consciousness-raising groups are basically rather warm places, with a lot of lightness and joking and positive energy under the sadness and oppression; while men's groups are basically rather sour and dour and low-energy places, with a lot of depression under the positive aims.

## Minzies and Frongs

The reason for this is not hard to seek. And I like to illustrate it with a story about two races of creatures called the Minzies and the Frongs. The Minzies are very thin, with tall pointed heads, and eyes near the top of their heads. They have very feeble little legs, rather oddly bowed, so that they find it quite painful to walk any distance. They have long, powerful arms and very sensitive fingers, so that they are very good at reaching and manipulating and moving things.

The Frongs, on the other hand, have very powerful legs, which carry them across the country at great speed for long

*Figure 2  A Minzie on a Frong*

distances, and enable them to spend all day on their feet, if necessary. But they have little squat upper bodies, short weak arms and rather poor eyesight, so they cannot see very far or do complex things with their hands.

These two races have developed a symbiotic relationship, whereby the Minzies ride around on the shoulders of the Frongs, who have necks and shoulders shaped in such a way as to make this very easy. The Frongs carry the Minzies around all day, the Minzies seeing ahead, guiding and manipulating, and the Frongs providing the support, energy and endurance.

The Minzies don't think much of the Frongs, rather looking down on them. They have sayings like 'Wine, singing and Frongs' – indicating that it doesn't much matter which one you've got, as long as you've got one.

Frongs, on the other hand, look up to Minzies, and take a great interest in what they are doing, thinking and feeling. They even boast slightly about their Minzies – 'My Minzie is heavier than yours' – and so on.

Now when they have separate meetings to discuss their feelings and their experience, the content of the Frongs' meetings is all rather unpleasant and serious, because they complain about all their ill-treatment by the Minzies and their secondary, service role in the community, but the underlying feeling is rather cheerful and relaxed, because they haven't got a Minzie sitting on them, and it's quite a relief.

When the Minzies have a meeting, on the other hand, the topics are all very positive and interesting – all about things they've achieved, new sights they have seen, and so on. But the underlying tone is one of sadness and loss, because they haven't got a Frong to sit on. They often try to sit on each other, but they're the wrong shape for that, and it doesn't work very well.

Now of course these are purely imaginary creatures, and the analogies with us are not very close, but the flavour is unmistakable. Men's groups don't last as long as women's groups, and have a higher turnover than women's groups. There have never been many men's groups, in comparison with the number of women's groups. And the reason is simple – the women are going to gain freedom and the men are going to lose freedom, or what usually feels to them like freedom.

## Freedom

The word 'freedom', as used by men, needs some careful watching. It is often quite oppressive in a curious way, as Mann (1975) once pointed out.

I'd like to give an example of this, from a workshop on sex roles which I co-led in the north of England. One man in the group, a young guy with long hair and a tie-dye T-shirt, had professed himself to be a lover of freedom and a supporter of the women's movement. Now one of the things my co-leader and I had noticed was that the men in this group were talking more than the women. So the next time that talking came around, we distributed ten slips of paper to each person, and said that each time someone spoke, they would put a slip in the middle. No one could speak any more once all their slips had gone. This was an idea taken from a feminist group, who according to Ti-Grace Atkinson had found it a good way to deal with the voluble and the silent. And in this instance the intention was to give the women more chance to talk, instead of the men doing most of the talking. But we didn't tell the group this, because we wanted people to experience the difference before talking about it.

What happened was instructive. The man already mentioned got very angry about being given a rule or structure so restrictive, and in the name of freedom threw away his slips, made a longish speech about rules in the group being just like oppressive structures outside the group, and provoked a political discussion which was carried on almost entirely between the men in the group. After about an hour of this (this was a weekend group) with a lot of raised voices and red faces, one of the women asked my co-leader what the point of the slips was. When she explained the point, a great silence fell.

This shows how the idea of freedom can be just as conditioned by the distortions of patriarchy as any other idea. The man here thought he was resisting the patriarchal authority when in fact he was actually being the patriarchal authority. People today are much more alert to this kind of thing than they were a few years ago, and much less inclined to take would-be rebels at their face value.

To put this another way, we might say that this man was consciously libertarian, but unconsciously authoritarian. And this idea of an unconscious dimension to the political struggle became much more important after 1976.

# CHAPTER 3

# Second channel of healing

It was in 1975 that a whole new dimension appeared in my relationship with feminism in the person of my wife. I had been working in my therapy (which now included co-counselling, as well as all the groups I had been going to, and my self-directed LSD trips) on various aspects of a horrible female figure I called Big Granny, who was full of hate for me.

In April I had a long therapy session where I quite spontaneously went back to my own birth and relived it, discovering that I had hated being born, hated being weaned, and hated my mother for separating from me. I had decided to get revenge on my mother, and all the hate I had experienced from my Big Granny fantasy figure was actually my own hate, projected into the outside world.

I had resolved, it became gradually clear over the ensuing months, to be independent, to not need women or anyone else, and to get revenge on my mother. This desire for revenge had spread and spread until it included all women and all men too. In reality, I hated everyone. But in particular, and most of all, I hated my wife.

Through the therapy, I was now able to give this up. I was able to forgive my mother, and to forgive myself for making such a mistake. My whole attitude to women started to melt and change, and this was very noticeable to the women I met after that.

When I told my wife that I had made this amazing discovery,

that deep down I hated her, and was in effect using her to get revenge on my mother, she expressed no surprise, except that it had taken me so long to discover it.

But although this breakthrough did not affect my relationship with my wife, it had a powerful effect on everything else. It released a whole flood of energy which enabled me to write two books that year, to write articles for two new magazines which came out that year, to do intensive work with the Red Therapy group, to devise a whole new style of workshop with John Southgate called *Dialectics as a felt experience*, to run and take part in a number of other group workshops, and to sunbathe in the garden in the lovely Summer weather. It all felt very easy and unpressured. It felt like the best year of my life so far. I was 50.

## Unconsciousness raising

One of the main discoveries of psychotherapy – not just psycho-analysis, but also every kind of therapy which actually works in any depth – is that it isn't possible to change self-defeating patterns of action just by wanting to. You have to be prepared to work on them in some indirect way, being very aware of what may lie behind or underneath a particular feeling or action. Often breaking one pattern helps a lot in breaking others.

So the idea came of pairs or groups of people getting together in such a way that any individual can say – 'I can't seem to lead my political life properly because such and such a bit of my behaviour seems to get in the way.' In 1975 I wrote an article which appeared in the radical psychology magazine *Humpty Dumpty* under the title 'Political Therapy'. It said – 'Perhaps we could work politically in a more effective way if we began to work at the unconscious level.' Later this idea became more popular, and by 1978 a number of people were talking about unconsciousness raising as a complement to the familiar con-sciousness raising.

In the Red Therapy group, and later in Alternative Socialism, this actually started to happen. I saw a man confronted by a group of women for two hours, and then being helped by gestalt therapy into a kind of amazing vision of what it would be like to be a non-sexist person – and actually becoming like a real human being. I saw a woman suddenly seeing that by consistently rejecting women and female things she was rejecting herself, and opening up to the realisation of what it would be like to value herself as a woman. I saw a woman role-playing a man in relation to two other women, and successfully manipulating them for half an hour in the face of every effort they made to achieve an honest encounter with 'him'. These were powerful and moving experiences for me, and taught me that politics and therapy were not necessarily alien or distant one from another.

It does not mean that we should stop work at the conscious level. There are still the same enormous tasks to be done there. All that it means is that, since many of the things we want to question and change were accepted by us early in life, and then the knowledge of that acceptance was repressed, those things are in us in a very deep and important way, which we cannot overcome by conscious effort alone.

## Models of therapy

The two models of therapy which came up in the 1970s were co-counselling and the self-help group. In both of these cases there is no expert who is 'there' already, and who just needs to be emulated or learned from. Both of them are able to get into unconscious material. For these models to work politically it seems that what is necessary is for the motivation to be political. As a cartoon in the Red Therapy (1978) pamphlet put it – 'I just ain't gonna be much help in smashing the system because the system is doing a pretty good job of smashing me.'

Co-counselling came to Britain in the early 1970s via a sociologist named Tom Scheff (Evison and Horobin, 1983) who had been involved with Re-Evaluation Counselling as developed by

Harvey Jackins (1965). The network spread quickly, and by 1975 there were already two breakaway groups who resented the tight control from Seattle. The basic idea is that two people meet once a week (or however often suits them) for two hours (or however long they want or can manage) and that for the first half of the time A is the client and B the counsellor, while for the second half of the time B is the client and A the counsellor. There is no mystification, because they have both learned the same techniques, often from the same person at the same time. There is no authority or expert problem, because the relationship is equal in its basic assumptions. And no money changes hands, which eliminates another source of imbalance.

There are of course some costs for the training, but even this can be overcome by one-to-one teaching, and one school of co-counselling even brought out a self-training manual (Southgate and Randall, 1978) which can be used by two people or a group without a teacher.

Co-counselling has always appealed to politically minded people, and indeed one of the nicest books on it is entitled *How to Change Yourself and Your World*. The Harvey Jackins organisation has produced a number of magazines specially addressed to blacks, to women, to handicapped people, to teachers and so on, exhibiting a real social conscience and desire to reach out to such groups. On at least one occasion they have even brought out a magazine addressed to men.

Self-help groups have of course existed for many years, and some of these, such as Alcoholics Anonymous, are well known and widespread. Consciousness-raising groups became one of the main ways of working in the women's liberation movement from the late 1960s onwards. But of course they were only for women, and they only occasionally involved any therapy. It was not until the 1970s that therapy started to be used in women's groups (Ernst and Goodison, 1981). Men's groups of course started later, but they very quickly found that therapy was necessary if they were to get anywhere. One of the places where this awareness was hammered out was in the Red Therapy group. This was a mixed group, but after a year or two it often divided into two – a women's group and a men's group – and this split eventually took over from the mixed group and replaced it. So a great deal was learned before the group came to an end.

## Red Therapy

How does therapy work in a men's group? Some examples from the Red Therapy group may help to make it clear.

One man came to the men's group feeling very bruised because a woman he had really depended on left him, saying at one point that 'there's nothing there'. In the group he became more aware of how unresponsive he had been with her, withdrawing from arguments, never talking about feelings, never even having any feelings very much. The group encouraged him to get in touch with his feelings, and to his surprise he found he did have feelings after all. Pain, grief, joy, anger – they were all there, but he had been afraid to feel them. They were frozen, blocked. So the woman had been right and wrong at the same time.

Many men are blocked in this way, because our whole culture discourages men from expressing emotion. For a brief period at the end of the 1960s it looked as if things were changing: articles were published in big-circulation magazines with titles like – 'It's OK to cry in the office' – but the 1970s and 1980s have seen a gradual return to hardness. This is particularly serious for men, because the kind of half-person who results from the cutting-off of feelings is dangerous, both to himself (Jourard, 1974) and to others (Easlee, 1983).

The reason why therapy is necessary to deal with this problem is that the reasons why men lock up their feelings very often go back far into childhood, back into the time when we can't remember anything. This means that good resolutions and even gentle encouragement are not enough; early pain has to be faced and worked through.

Another reason is that even if early experience doesn't come into it, feeling good emotions and feeling bad emotions are part of the same deal – you don't get one without the other (though many men do try to have just good feelings without the bad ones). So as soon as a man really starts opening up the world of his feelings, it is the ones which have been most firmly pushed down or set aside which come up with the most force, and these are the most painful ones. It is the disowned feelings which are the most necessary to recover – to fill up the holes in the person, as it were – and the most difficult to deal with. That is why they were disowned in the first place.

The discoveries which are made in therapy are often very simple and banal, and sound quite obvious or unimportant when written down. 'My mother didn't really love me.' 'I didn't really love my mother.' 'I didn't kill my sister.' 'I do have a right to exist.' But when they are genuinely discovered and deeply felt, they may unlock a whole lifetime of locked-up feelings, and enable the man to give up his myth – his story about his life, which he uses to hold everything in place and stop it changing.

Another example. A man in one group complained that he felt pressured by his work, his political activities, his relationships and all the rest. There seemed to be no end to them, and they overwhelmed him. The other men in the group scattered boots, shoes, scarves, coats, bags and gloves round the floor, each representing one activity named by the man. Eventually the process came to an end. The man then looked round at all the pieces and started grouping them together. He was then encouraged to give priorities to them. In this process some conflicts emerged, and he was encouraged to work through these conflicts to see where they came from. He was then able to eliminate some of the activities altogether, and explore his feelings about that. Others could be grouped together in ways which made more sense and gave him more space. By the end he felt greatly relieved.

This is the sort of thing which men often need to do, particularly if they tend to take on many new activities in an active way, as many politically minded men do. Often some very fundamental issues emerge, as for example between one part of the man which wants to do more and more, and another part which resists that, in a seemingly weak or childish way. Often it turns out that this is a very deep split in the man, between a false self disguised as a competent and forceful ego, and a real self disguised as an incompetent and passive inner child. This can then be worked through quite well by using any one of a number of different therapy approaches (Rowan, 1983).

Another example. Five men are listening to one man talking about responsibility – how he feels oppressed by the responsibility of his job, his wife, his new baby. As he is encouraged to go into this and to really explore the feelings involved, it raises painful memories, suddenly emerging, of when he was a child. His father died when he was only 10, and he felt that too much responsibility had dropped on him then – it produced feelings of panic in him, which came back in the therapy group. Going back into these old feelings, and doing justice to them, seems to make the present situation easier to sort out.

Here we can see one of the major uses of therapy – to sort out a painful experience from an experience of Pain (Janov and Holden, 1977). A painful experience is something in the world which does actually cause real pain, which usually has a beginning, a middle and an end. It starts, we feel it; it finishes, we let go of it and carry on. But an experience of Pain is an old tape, as it were, playing continually inside us, and whenever something in the world reminds us of it, it plays its old tune at full volume all over again. We keep it going because it seems important to our whole picture of who we are.

Now most of the unpleasant experiences we have in our lives are a mixture of these two. On the one hand there is the real current pain and on the other there is the neurotic Pain. They combine to make our felt experience and we can't tell them apart. So it feels to us as if it is a really terrible experience, whereas from the outside it just looks like a rather bad experience. Now what therapy does is to separate these two things out, and to deal with the neurotic Pain on its own, transforming it in some way so that the energy locked up in storing and playing the old tape can be used for something better. The person is then left with just the real current experience to deal with, and that makes the whole thing much more possible. (There are of course other models of how therapy works, but I find this one generally useful.)

Another example. Six men are sitting on cushions in a front room in Dalston. One of them is talking about the feelings he has when driving a car – how he feels powerful and wants to overtake everything. He is encouraged to explore this, and it turns into an increasingly dramatic fantasy about driving red sports cars, meeting sexy blondes and ruling the world. He becomes so obnoxious and superior that the rest of the group eventually climb all over him and sit on top of him, thus demonstrating the power of collective action.

This is using the 'groupness' of the group in a very simple but effective way, just allowing something to develop and grow until it changes into its opposite. That particular man, who happened to be me, has never been able to think of cars in quite the same way again. And this is very close to the whole character of the oppressive male ego, which needs to be challenged so often.

One time in the Red Therapy group I deliberately asked the women to challenge and confront me, so that I could change further. What they said, and the way they said it, threw me back into a primal (a cathartic experience where repressed material comes up very intensely) where my father was saying to me – 'You can come with me if you're good enough – but you're not good enough.' This was another breakthrough, because I suddenly saw that I didn't need to live up to an image of myself originally derived from my father. I didn't need to take care of my ego.

### The healthy male ego

One of the most striking phrases which hit me in the early days of men's groups was – *The 'healthy male ego' is oppressive and sick.*

At first it seemed merely insulting and unhelpful – the sort of thing that some women might find useful to come out with but not much good to me. But the work in anti-sexist therapy has made it clear that this is in fact a sober truth which needs to be dealt with very seriously.

In therapy, we are continually trying to get at the truth behind appearances. And if you do this for a while, you eventually get a very keen eye for the phony – you develop a good crap-detector. And it really does seem as if most of what passes for straightforward male qualities is quite phony.

For example, every study ever done of men shows that they tend to be aggressive. They are competitive, argumentative, pushy and so on (Brothers, 1982). But when we allow men in group therapy to express their anger and aggression, we find that underneath it are a lot of feelings of inferiority and weakness, which are much harder to admit to. This became so obvious in one piece of work done by a man in the group that we called the whole syndrome the Samurai and the Slob.

This man said that in challenging situations he felt like one of the samurai – the legendary warriors of ancient Japan. He felt poised, centred, warlike, cool and ready for action. He could threaten and get his own way. But if the challenge was countered, if the other side fought back, he then felt completely beaten and weak, and collapsed into a slob. This sudden switch from samurai to slob came up often in that and in other groups which I attended later. It usually related to early stuff about the father. Now I am not saying that this is true of all men, simply that it came up surprisingly often, and very often with men who had good records of strong political action.

But the roots of aggression can go deeper than this. Some of my own self-exploration leads me to accept the view of Cynthia Adcock (1982) that the common root of sexism and militarism is fear of the 'Other', and originally fear of the mother. She points out that the infant is vulnerable and helpless in relation to the mother, and very easily feels any withdrawal or absence of the mother as a rejection. So the mother holds a terrible and arbitrary power:

The power, the immediate power over the infant, was female. We cannot help but live in fear, in dread, for any power on which we are so deeply dependent. In this fact, I think, lies the origin of sexism. Torn from the mother by birth, needy for her milk and love, we feel a terrified ambivalence toward her.

Again I am not saying that this is true of all men, but it was certainly true for me. It was not until I dealt with my deepest feelings about my mother that I could give up my project of getting revenge on her, which had spread and spread until I had a sort of hatred for all women and all men, too.

I remember an incident when, soon after I had had the primal session where I had broken through my need to destroy my mother, and forgiven her, and forgiven myself, I met a very strong radical feminist, a working-class artist and mother whom I had seen up to now as a man-hater and male-eliminator. We talked easily and normally, and I expressed surprise at how little anger there was between us – it was all so peaceful. And she said, 'I never felt angry at you. All that stuff came from you.' That was amazing to hear, but when I considered it, it really was true.

And I believe that this is common too – that there are many men who see feminists as enemies and hostile, and who can find odd quotes here and there to support their contention that they are all man-haters and ball-breakers, when really it is their own hostility that is much more important and in need of attention. Underneath their self-assured normality and good sense lies the 'healthy male ego', and the healthy male ego is hostile towards women. Until we understand this much better, nothing much is going to change. But this understanding does not come at a head level, from reading books or going to meetings – it comes from personal change and development which is based on deeper self-knowledge of the kind which is achievable in a therapy group.

What we discovered in the Red Therapy group was that no highly qualified experts were needed for this. Self-help is sufficient. Two or three people in the original group had done quite a lot of therapy and did more of the therapeutic work in the group, but gradually others learned from them and from going to outside groups, until after two years virtually everyone felt able to make suggestions and work with someone who wanted attention; sometimes six or seven 'therapists' would weave in and out of the action, making suggestions, helping him or her to go a bit further, following where it led, without competing with each other and without getting in each other's way.

Perhaps it is important to say, however, that not only did people in the group go to outside groups led by experts in a particular technique, bringing that expertise back into the group, but that many – perhaps most – of the people in the group went on later to do further work on themselves with the help of professional practitioners. A group is very good for stimulating experiences and for stirring up a lot of material, but it is in one-to-one work that this material can be worked through more thoroughly and more deeply. And for some types of material, someone with good training and a lot of experience can be quite essential, if it is to be worked on successfully (see my chapter in Dryden, in press).

But from a feminist point of view, most of what needs to be done can be done in self-help groups and through co-counselling.

### Psychic celibacy

It was in this way that I discovered that particular quality of the healthy normal male ego which Bianchi (1976) calls psychic celibacy. He says this about it:

> placing woman in heaven (Mary) or hell (Eve) became a
> convenient way of removing her from earth where she could
> compete with men for a just share of material and human
> resources. . . . I have labelled this well-entrenched masculine
> mentality as psychic celibacy. Although distinct from physical
> celibacy as practiced in Catholicism, psychic celibacy is a

more pervasive and imposing phenomenon. It consists in keeping women mentally and emotionally at arms' length. It is in fact the core dogma of our patriarchal era. Woman can be exalted as wife, virgin, mother or deprecated (and enjoyed) as temptress, playmate, whore. In whatever way this male projection works, woman is object, non-equal, manipulated, distanced. . . . Such a world is profoundly celibate.

This seemed such a challenging view of men that I decided to investigate it more fully. I went into the literature, and discovered the striking paper by Ruth Hartley (1959) which shows how violently the male psyche is distorted by early socialisation. For example, she says:

a great many boys do give evidence of anxiety centred in the whole area of sex-connected role behaviours, an anxiety which frequently expresses itself in over-straining to be masculine, in virtual panic at being caught doing anything traditionally defined as feminine, and in hostility toward anything even hinting at 'femininity', including females themselves.

It is precisely this kind of panic which is most effective in producing neurotic defences of one kind and another, and moreover those which are most enduring and hard to change. And in case anyone thinks that those days are gone, someone told me recently of her son, who came home from school, aged 7, in tears because the other children had been teasing him about the occupation of his father – a male nurse. Couldn't his father please change his job, he wailed.

The difficulties are again made worse by the fact that the father is not at home nearly as much as the mother, in the majority of families. Often the boy never actually sees the father doing his real daily-life activities at all. So the information he gets about proper masculine behaviour is limited and distorted. There is plenty of information on television, but it is hard to distinguish between fact and fiction, and media images are in any case highly selected in the direction of reinforcing existing stereotypes, in the vast majority of cases. The main source of information for boys is, therefore, the peer group of other boys. But since they have no better sources of information than he has, all they can do is to pool the impressions and anxieties they derived from their early training. Ruth Hartley ends her paper by saying:

> When he sees women as weak, easily damaged, lacking strength in mind and body, able to perform only the tasks which require the least strength and are of least importance, what boy in his right senses would not give his all to escape this alternative to the male role? For many, unfortunately, the scramble to escape takes on all the aspects of panic, and the outward semblance of non-femininity is achieved at a tremendous cost of anxiety and self-alienation. From our data, we would infer that the degree of anxiety experienced has a direct relation to the degree of pressure to be 'manly' exerted on the boy, the rigidity of the pattern to which he is pressed to conform, the availability of a good model, and the apparent degree of success which his efforts achieve.

The results of this process are easy to pick up. As Sexton (1969) has said, the research shows that children have already picked up their dislike for the woman's role by the age of 4. By kindergarten about half the girls prefer the father's role and about a quarter of the boys prefer the mother's role. By 12 or 13, girls who act like boys are much more socially accepted than boys who act like girls. Among adults, 20–31 per cent of women prefer the male social role, while only 2–4 per cent of men prefer the woman's role. Role theory is full of material like this.

Psychoanalysis digs even deeper into the roots of psychic celibacy. Robert Seidenberg (1973) says this:

> Although it is a vast oversimplification to attribute mental illness to one cause, we are becoming aware of social forces

that filter down to the family and mother–child unit. The
effects of a male-dominated society on 'mothering' cannot
be overlooked as potentially and actually disintegrative. . . .
In the unconscious of men as found in psychoanalysis, there
is a deep-seated fear and loathing of women. All the songs
of love do not displace this underlying contempt for those
'unfortunates' with gaping wounds where a penis ought to
be. It is the loathing of differences that encourages and
maintains the male homosexual culture from which females
are regularly excluded.

The difference between an enlightened Freudian like this and a
humanistic psychologist is that we don't see any of this as
inevitable. It is because the 'fear and loathing' is permitted and
encouraged by a million social forms that it becomes powerful.
If it were denied by the culture, it would become an individual
quirk with few consequences.

But at least this makes it clear that when feminists are accused
of man-hating they are quite right to come back and say that
the general culture of society is woman-hating, and that this is
the major problem.

Not that it is only women who are seeing the breakdown of
patriarchy as a key political issue. Men too have seen the need
for change as something which affects them in positive ways.
Books like those of Korda (1972), Farrell (1975), Goodman and
Walby (1975) and Hodson (1984) all see that the change is one
which is badly needed if men are to be whole persons, and not
fragmented and one-sided apologies for human beings.

My own investigations, brief and preliminary as they were,
showed very definitely that men have very deep problems in
relating to women in any adequate way. They find intimacy
very hard. Opening up to a woman is a rare and risky process.
Some of what I found is expressed very succinctly in this case
study from Swenson (1973):

As the counselling progressed, it became apparent that one
personification the husband had of his wife was as a kind

of witch who was trying to consume and control him totally, while the wife viewed her husband as a totally self-centred man who refused to give any affection or consideration to her or the children. The wife's efforts to gain attention and affection were experienced by the husband as attempts to consume and control. The husband's efforts to protect himself from total control by his wife were experienced by the wife as a self-centred withdrawal from the family.

This is one classic pattern. Others were found by George Bach (Bach and Wyden, 1969) who discovered that the vast majority of the 'good' marriages he studied were either card-house marriages (a false front rather precariously held up and maintained) or game-playing marriages where control was more important than intimacy.

Self-protection is the name of the game in this whole area. So many of the quotes in the Hite Report (1981) give this flavour:

> Sometimes my girlfriend gets upset with me because I don't talk to her or don't express myself. Sometimes I am quiet and don't feel like talking – usually I feel alienated or mad at her for something at these times, but I hate to admit that. Especially to her. I feel a loss of self-respect when I get emotional, especially if I get mad. I don't like to admit that she can make me mad. It's like she has power over me because she makes me feel excited, aroused, nervous, insecure, wonderful, and confused, all at the same time. It seems humiliating.

So in order to save themselves from humiliation, men erect this barrier around themselves, and keep women at arms' length emotionally and mentally. (Some of this material is taken from Rowan, 1979.)

In therapy and research, then, the problems come out very clearly and in depth. But what, then, emerges in the way of solutions to these problems?

# CHAPTER 4

# Penis and power

My life was coming to a crisis. Although in my therapy I had had this breakthrough about women, and my relationships with women were easier and more fruitful, my relationship with my wife was worse than ever. In the Red Therapy group, which devoted a lot of time to relationships, I worked on many dreams, and came to the conclusion that my wife's criticisms of me were partly feminist – and from those I could and should learn – but were also partly personal and destructive. One very striking dream seemed to be about castration – of me, by her. So I decided to get out.

But 1977 was a terrible year economically for me. My interests had moved away from market research into therapy and organisation development, but my main income had always come from market research, which at my level was a very well-paid job. There were few organisational jobs about, because of the recession, and I had no place to do therapy, except the odd weekend group at various centres.

Of course this economic climate affected men generally. But it was one of the paradoxes of the 1970s that while it was a very bad time for the dreams of the 1960s and a very shattering time for any ideas of revolutionary change, it was a very good time for the growth of feminism. A much deeper and broader understanding of what feminism meant was prevalent, and laws were being passed, rules were being changed, centres were being set up – the whole thing was growing. I met one man whose job it was to go through every handbook issued for training purposes by the Post Office, removing the sexism from the words and pictures; a huge task, and one which was being carried out very thoroughly.

In 1978 there was a resurgence of the men's movement. A conference took place in London, attended by about 150 men, which was very encouraging on the whole. It saw the publication of a new magazine called *Achilles Heel,* produced by the same collective which had brought out Paul Morrison's moving book of poems entitled *Pregnant Fatherhood* the year before. In the summer there was a men's camp, and in Manchester a series of meetings on men's politics. In London a new men's centre was started in Islington.

In April 1979, after a disconcerting change of date, there was a national conference – really the first one ever – and about 300 men attended. This was the biggest turnout yet, and the event was successful, and the heart began to come back into the movement. Another issue of *Achilles Heel* came out just in time for the conference, and there was a lot of good feeling around. The pamphlet *Red Therapy* was talked about a lot at this conference, because it seemed to show how men's groups fitted in to the whole picture of the relationship between politics and therapy.

## Commitments

In 1980 there was another big conference, this time in Bristol, and here there was a lot of talk about what came to be known as the Ten Commitments. These were drawn up by a group of men including Keith Motherson, who felt that the men's movement was too vague about its relationship to women and the women's movement. They wanted men to commit themselves to some definite undertaking to support feminist ideas and practice, spelt out in some detail (see Box 1).

At the Bristol conference, the men there seemed to feel that this set of commitments was too pushy and premature. There

**Box 1 – Notes and riders towards ten commitments**

1 *Commitment to the group* – men against sexism politics recognised as important, not a hobby or poor-relation political commitment – gripfulness – thought between meetings – consideration for our brothers expressed in punctuality, regularity, consistency, giving reasons for non-attendance or leaving – holding together through difficult patches – switchboarding and introducing new members well – being able to count on each other to do what they say they'll do between meetings.

2 *Consciousness-raising done rigorously* – intimacy and risk – based on personal experience and gut feelings (therapy and bodywork necessary often) – generalising from shared experience – cumulation of insights into male conditioning, patriarchal culture – CR as central and continuing, not just parallel to or prior to action, but linked to it and nourished by it.

3 *Support for the Women's Liberation Movement* – creches, food preparation, duplicating, fundraising where requested – sharing of money – support for campaigns, protests – hassling to communicate with men referred to us by anti-rape groups – not letting putdowns of women past in everyday life without a struggle, e.g. with men at work, on the street, in pubs.

4 *Support for Gay Liberation* and our self-liberation as gay – support for gay struggles against heterosexist oppression – wearing gay badge – acknowledging exclusive heterosexuality as a deep hangup imposed by patriarchal society, not 'biologically given' – social links with the gay community.

5 *Sharing childcare* – both in the routines of our lives and in connection with men's events, camps, outings, etc. – availability for babysitting – links with Women's Aid houses – becoming 'goddessfathers' to children of friends – raising issues about respect for children and childcare in other contexts, events.

6 *Learning from gay and feminist culture* – reading literature, studying theory together, films/theatre/art/music/dance – in turn contributing to a gyn-androus, feminist-identified people's culture from our own specific experience as men.

7 *Action on our own behalf* – devised independently but, where necessary, 'cleared' with women's or gay movement – questioning publicly the value of patriarchal assumptions and instructions concerning being men – men and work campaigns for part-time, flexi-time, shared work and paternity leave – men and medical matters action, etc.

8 *Propaganda and outreach programmes* (linked to actions) to reach specific groups of men, especially ones who haven't heard of Men Against Sexism and whose experience we are in need of to complement our own – use of media – making our own pamphlets, leaflets, films, plays, etc. – not being a closed 'in-group'.

9 *Link-ups with other Men Against Sexism groups* locally, regionally, nationally, through special interest groups, etc. – participating in and dialogue with more general men's groups – links where welcome with women's and gay movements, readiness to support their leads in wider political culture.

10 *Renunciation of violence* (physical, emotional and verbal) towards women and oppressed people, children, etc. – cultivation of a nonviolent spirit in negotiation of differences with women, gay people and brothers in Men Against Sexism groups – not interrupting, listening, not caricaturing opposing arguments deliberately, etc. – not intimidating people with displays of anger when crossed – asking forgiveness when we violate others and where relevant making restitution.

is a definite whiff about it of the guilt-inducing 1974 argument, because it seemed that hardly any men were even doing the first item on the list, never mind any of the others. It was as if the list of 'shoulds' induced apathy rather than enthusiasm, as nagging usually does. If the 'commitments' had been pushed through at the conference, as perhaps they might have been, another collapse of the movement might have been predicted. But rescue came in the shape of an alternative statement drawn up by Paul Morrison (later published in several places) which met with almost unanimous approval from the assembly. It seems worthwhile to give it in full here, because it is the nearest thing to a manifesto which has come out of the struggle to define a male anti-sexism (see Box 2).

It can be seen that the 'minimum self-definition' and the 'ten commitments' are not far apart, and what they have in common is the heartland of the men's movement. They both see the necessity of therapy as a part of the process, for example. It seemed that at last we had a clear statement of identity and a better sense of purpose to go with it. And for a while it did seem as if this worked. Some of the strongest and best issues of *Achilles Heel* began to come out, now concentrating on one theme per issue – No. 4 on *Men and Work,* No. 5 on *Masculinity and Violence* and Nos 6/7 on *Sexuality*. Some good issues of the *Anti-Sexist Newsletter* came out at the same time.

But quite soon it became obvious that all was not well. Newsletters came out more haltingly, no more big conferences were held (there was a small one in Manchester and another small one in London) and the intervals between one issue of *Achilles Heel* and another also became longer. The reasons for this became clearer in the Summer of 1983, when the *Newsletter* printed seventeen pages on Accountability. This magic word Accountability turned out to be the Commitments writ large, and with much stronger undertones. The argument was basically a simple one, and went as follows:

Despite our differences we are united in our support of those women who argue that men against sexism should be

**Box 2 – A minimum definition of the anti-sexist men's movement**

This conference of men places itself unequivocally in support of the women's and gay movements in the struggle against sexism. We realise that men's power in our society means that we are not an equivalent or 'parallel' movement. We are certainly not a competitive one.

Yet we have discovered that the power we have over women and other men also cripples and distorts our own lives. Learning how to give up this control and grow out of our masculine straitjackets is a frightening but very positive process.

We are traditionally expected to be unemotional, tough, aggressive, individualistic and not to admit weakness. Yet we all contain the opposite qualities – gentleness, co-operativeness, lovingness, receptiveness, which we can reclaim and allow.

The main vehicle for our personal changes has been men's groups, in which we can look at our negative patterns of relating to women and other men.

Becoming close to and drawing support from other men reduces the exclusive emotional burden that men have traditionally placed upon women. Recently some men have found therapy and co-counselling valuable tools in helping to resolve deep patterns and oppressive blocks in themselves.

We want to change our relationships with children, to take our full and equal share of responsibility for childcare. We have been discovering the positive benefits of being close to and learning from children. This means looking to change patterns of work and pay that are dominant in our society, and confronting eventually the huge gulf between the workplace and domestic labour and life.

The main public expression so far of our support for the women's liberation movement has been in helping to organise creches for women's events, and in attending mixed demonstrations. We would like to find other ways of supporting women's movement campaigns and demands, when invited, and in developing the particular contribution we can make as men – for example, in confronting rape and male violence, and in support of a woman's right to choose, equal pay, adequate nursery provision, and so forth.

The many of us who are heterosexual are committed to exploring our prejudices against gay men and lesbians, and our fear of our own gay feelings. We would like to find ways of linking up with and supporting the Gay Liberation Movement and specific gay movement campaigns.

We have been developing ways of reaching out to other men, and confronting the sexism that we meet in other men in our lives and workplaces. We want to create a positive anti-sexist culture that men can draw support from in their changes.

We want to develop campaigns in our own interest as anti-sexist men – against media stereotypes of men, around unemployment, men's health, for well-paid part-time work, for job-sharing, paternity leave, etc.

Patriarchal culture has become synonymous with the 'conquering' of the natural environment. We want to live in harmony with the natural world, including our own bodies, and to redirect our skills and technologies in such directions as to make this harmony possible, eliminating poverty and enabling each individual to live to her or his fullest potential.

We realise that in our society sexism is inextricably linked with class and racial oppression, and with imperialism. We are working towards a society free of all these.

The anti-sexist men's movement is small in number, and it is young. We are only now beginning to feel confident to move out of relative isolation. We need to recognise our limitations, *as well as our very real strengths*.

In coming to take collective political initiatives, we don't want to create new hierarchies of leaders and led.

accountable to women and the Women's Liberation
Movement, and we are concerned to explore ways of putting
this commitment into practice. We want to challenge the
assumption that men are anti-sexist just because we call
ourselves anti-sexist. We want to see the development of a
genuine anti-sexist practice among men which is clear and
constructive in response to women's demands. And we want
to see men begin to give up the power and privilege we gain
at women's expense, and to challenge the power and
privileges of other men.

This is the guilt-provoking attack which was so effective nine
years before. Only now the whole thing is dressed up in a much
more sophisticated outfit. The authors take up the question of
guilt, saying that 'Guilt is largely a place of total inaction. It
sucks in energy and usually hangs on to the status quo like grim
death. However for me there is a positive place for guilt in that
it can cut through complacency.' They also take up the question
of therapy:

> It is not the concept of therapy, massage or male support I
> am criticising – indeed I think they can be very effective ways
> of us becoming clearer about our feelings and motivations.
> What I am critical of is the frequent complete absence of
> how they relate to changing the nature of male power in us,
> in other men and in male dominated institutions. I suspect
> that they often encourage the further development of male
> bonding between sensitive men and as a result support male
> power and are not anti-sexist.

But for all the appearance of taking difficulties into account,
and doing justice to possible objections, the message is the same
in the end:

> We are often too afraid to confront, to challenge and to
> criticise other men for fear of disrupting 'the brotherhood'
> and of being labelled competitive, heavy, a politico, or simply

divisive. And when we do challenge this 'brotherhood' it is seen by other men as a threat to the creation of trust and honesty among men, or a form of guilt-tripping. I firmly believe that this is a defensive reaction on the part of men who wish to avoid criticism and, ultimately, to avoid women's demands on men to take responsibility for our behaviour. And this is why 'anti-sexist' men have seldom *publicly* criticised other men about their misogyny, or challenged the institutions of male supremacy and violence.

The point is that, whatever the truth of this position, and whatever its acceptability to feminist women, it simply paralyses men. They are not energised and made more potent in their anti-sexism by this kind of message.

And I think the reason for this is that it secretly implies a total repudiation of all that is masculine or male. Indeed, the repudiation is not even that secret: one of the quotes in boxes which decorate this issue of the *Newsletter* is from our old friend John Stoltenberg, who we met in Chapter 2. It says:

> To take seriously in one's 'consciousness' the fact of sexist injustice would have to mean for men, as it already does for many women, *a total repudiation of masculinity*. All 'Men's Liberation' which in form and content is masculinity-*confirming*, is thus an escalation and permutation of masculinist aggression.

Now this really says that there is no place for a man, no place for a man at all, in a feminist world.

### The good penis

Although I have been telling this story as if it were history and external, there is also the internal story of how all this affected me. Around 1978 I was really very occupied with the whole issue of sexuality and male violence. It was this coercive violence which ultimately underlay all the less obvious ways in which women were put down by men. A brilliant article by Kokopeli and Lakey (1982) had the memorable sentence which really came home to me – 'Rape is the end logic of masculine sexuality.' Rape, they said, is not so much a sexual act as an act of violence expressed in a sexual way.

In this way some of the feminists I knew were seeing rape as in some way the key to the whole patriarchal edifice (Brownmiller, 1976), and at the same time the ultimate insult to women. As the ultimate insult it deserved the ultimate appropriate punishment – castration. There seemed to be something in the thought of castrating rapists which made the feminist spirit rise: there was a badge which came out about this time which showed a picture of an axe with blood dripping from it and the words 'Disarm Rapists'. But it also made sense at a more thought-out level. Mary Daly (1973) said:

> The method of liberation, then, involves a *castrating* of language and images that reflect and perpetuate the structure of a sexist world. It castrates precisely in the sense of cutting away the phallocentric value system imposed by patriarchy [which] ... has amounted to a kind of gang rape of minds as well as bodies. ... Now [we] are rising up to castrate not people but *the system* that castrates – that great 'God-Father' of us all which indulges senselessly and universally in the politics of rape.

These are strong words, which make a strong appeal to some women who I see as being very central to feminism and what it stands for. But they make me scared, because the feeling that comes through is that, if this talk of castration goes on long enough, it is *my* penis which is going for the chop. (Technical note: Castration strictly means removal of the testicles, but at an unconscious level, as many therapists of different persuasions have found, it means also removal of the whole penis.)

It seems to me that this image of castration may inspire some women, but it cannot be accepted by men. It is too close and too personal, and much too threatening.

But if that is the case, what can men see as their hope, their function, their role in a feminist world, or a post-patriarchal world? I got the clue from something very personal which happened to me.

In my therapy I had started to criticise my father's attitude to sex and to women. I became convinced that he really hated women and wanted to punish them with his penis. I was angry that all his attitudes to sex and to women were power-oriented, patriarchal. I acted out a scene where I tore his penis (his bad, exploitative, aggressive penis) right off and stuffed it down his throat.

Later I started to see that it was part of me myself that I was trying to get rid of – my own bad penis, my own hostile attitudes, my own power orientation. But what was I going to have instead? The prospect of not having a penis at all seemed unacceptable and in any case unrealistic and inappropriate. (The idea of having a cunt or a womb never came up at this point. That is just a fact about my experience and my consciousness at this time. But even if it had, I don't think my experience would have been so very different.)

One answer seemed to be the idea of having a nicey-nicey penis, which would never do anyone any harm. (To anyone who hasn't been in therapy, I must apologise for how fantastic all this must seem, but therapy is a hothouse where we take our fantasies for real and pursue them to the end.) But the nicey-nicey penis seemed too sweet, too would-be-innocent, too totally determined by being the very opposite of the bad penis, like two ends of a line:

Bad penis ——————————— Nicey-nicey penis

Was the answer to move to the middle of the line, and be a bit of each, a compromise between the two?

The answer which came up was NO to this. There was another possibility, which emerged in a later session. I could have a good penis. This I saw as being strong and powerful, but non-oppressive. If the bad penis was like a bayonet, a pistol or a club, and the nicey-nicey penis was like a passive tassel or a glass tumbler, the good penis was like a bridge, a crane or a communication tower. It could genuinely reach out to people, connect with people and co-operate with people. And this seemed to be on another dimension to the first line, including both the assertiveness of the bad penis and the receptivity of the nicey-nicey penis, but not reducing to the one-sidedness of either of them. The line now turned into a triangle, like this:

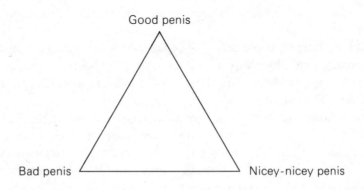

Putting this in terms which I feel happy with, but I know not everybody does, the bad penis was the thesis, the nicey-nicey penis was the antithesis, and the good penis the synthesis of the two. What all this meant to me in practice was that there was a good way of being a man, an OK way of having genuine male power that could be non-oppressive to women. I think I have to add here that I couldn't have arrived at this without having already worked through my very complicated feelings about loving and hating my mother, which I have described in an article elsewhere (Rowan, 1975). I was already a lot clearer about women when I began on this whole process.

So far this is all about me, and my experience in my own process of development. Is there a way of linking this in with anything more general, which possibly more people can relate to? Soon after all this happened, I remembered a theory I had come across, which also took a similar form. This stated that a very usual position for many people, perhaps the majority of

the human race, was powerlessness. People in this position feel
that they have no power, and do not exercise any power worth
talking about. Unless they move from this position, they are
never going to be able to take power over their own lives or
anything else.

Now one of the reasons why people do not move out of this
position is that they believe that there is only one kind of power:
power *over* people. That is, coercive power, autocratic power,
'masculine' power, potentially violent power – power which
rides roughshod over people, and makes them into inferiors. So
again we have a line:

Powerlessness ——————————————— Power over

If the choice is between being nice and powerless or nasty and
powerful, they would rather stick to being powerless. Sometimes
they try to go halfway along the line as a kind of compromise.

What the theory says (Fordyce and Weil, 1971) however, is
that this is a false choice, which wrongly dominates our thinking
about power, and paralyses us when we need to act. There is
another dimension to be brought in, which again gives us a
triangle. We can think and work in terms of power *with* other
people. (Again we can say if we like that powerlessness is the
thesis, power-over the antithesis, and power-with the synthesis,
because power-with gives us both the niceness and attractiveness
of powerlessness, together with the ability to get things done of
power-over.) We are now talking about the very powerful concept of social synergy, which Joanna Macy (1983) has written
about so eloquently – that is, making things happen by getting
together with other people in a co-operative way. This is a non-
oppressive kind of power which is able to get things done
without bringing up harmful feelings about inferiority and
superiority. It does not suppress leadership, but sees leadership
as something which all people can do at appropriate times.

Once we see power-with as an option, we are thereby enabled
to leave powerlessness behind much more easily. We don't need
to be afraid to leave our state of powerlessness, because there
is somewhere good to go to. We can exercise power without

being oppressors. When I remembered this theory, it occurred to me that it fitted with the triangle I had come to through the process of my own therapy:

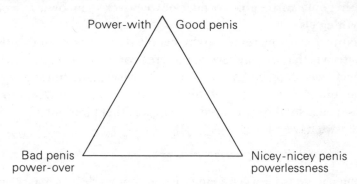

Power-with / Good penis

Bad penis
power-over

Nicey-nicey penis
powerlessness

And what it now means, as I see it, is that we now have a theory of power which is specifically relevant to men. Instead of shuffling hopelessly along a line where the only choice is between being harmful or harmless, we can go on to a positively good place, where we can define our own real strength in a non-patriarchal way. As Carl Rogers (1978) says, this is a revolutionary stance:

> My purpose in the whole first section of the book has been to show that a new politics of relationships is possible. From the intimacies of marriage to disputes between countries, there are living, effective examples of what a person-centred approach means in practice. In this new politics it has been discovered that the most powerful stance one can take in any relationship is, paradoxically, to leave responsible power in the hands of each person or each group.

And elsewhere in the same book he says that this means trusting the unconscious, trusting that our whole experience is more adequate than the intellect on its own – the very lesson which men have learned from therapy in our groups.

This also helps in seeing how we can relate to women. From

the power-over position, we can only relate to women as oppressors; from the powerlessness position, we can only relate to women as superior to us – we are underlings; but from the power-with position, we can relate in co-operative ways with any women who have got to a similar position in their own terms.

Again these theoretical matters tied in with my own life in practical ways. In 1978 I moved away from market research in a decisive way, first into organisational work and then, after further intensive training with Bill Swartley, into practising and teaching psychotherapy. And I made this work well enough economically so that I could afford to move away from my wife (my children were now grown-up) and set up a second home with a woman with whom I found I could have a genuinely intimate relationship. Such a good relationship is always a miracle, especially in the current appalling social, emotional and economic set-up, but it was a miracle I had worked for at two levels – the conscious and the unconscious.

And when I separated from my wife, after seven years of struggle, I found to my surprise that everyone approved. My wife found it a relief; my children thought it was long overdue; my mother thought it was a good thing; and my wife's mother thought it was a good idea. I felt myself as if a new chapter in my life could now begin.

What I believe is that the inner and the outer, the personal and the political, are basically one and the same. My own personal changes and the changes in the wider scene are not widely distant. This is why I believe it is worthwhile to bring in my own personal history – it may be highly relevant, in a number of ways, to what other people are going through. We all have to make changes, if the patriarchal world is going to change.

None of this is easy to do – we all have our various hangups which get in the way. But if the theory is any use, it can help us to see what directions to look in.

Armed with this fresh understanding, it became possible for me to look on questions like accountability in a way that escaped some of the criticisms. It meant that it was possible to be a man again, and to see that it was really nothing to do with castration. In fact, for the record, I am in one sense of the word castrated myself, in that in 1979 I had a vasectomy. It is now easier to see that I can be castrated and still be a man.

What was still difficult, however, was to get any kind of inkling at all of what this new kind of man was actually going to do. There seemed to be no models to follow. I couldn't find any good examples of men who had made it in a way which I could find inspiring. And in the end I had to go into a very strange place to find my model.

# CHAPTER 5

# *Androgyny*

But before we go on to that part of the work, there is a blind alley which must be explored. It is an important blind alley, and a very seductive blind alley, and particularly seductive to men.

In the Summer of 1980 I went to the Annual Meeting of the Association for Humanistic Psychology at Snowmass in Colorado. There were a couple of workshops on sex roles there, and as I went to them and talked to people I got more and more worried about the lack of political insight which I found there. The acute analysis of patriarchy, and the anger about it, which had come from the feminists seemed largely ignored. There was a kind of vague line which seemed to be floating around, which didn't seem to be written down anywhere, but which was just taken for granted. It seemed to be misleading, harmful, liberal, comforting and powerless. Later I found that it had been written down, after all.

### *Yin and Yang*

I had written it down myself, in an article which I had written the previous year (Rowan, 1980) and which, ironically, was published just before the annual meeting. It went like this:

> Instead of patriarchy what we want seems to be described as
> an androgynous or gynandrous society. Any human being

needs to have the ability to be active and passive, assertive and receptive, instrumental and expressive, tough and tender, strong and vulnerable, independent and sociable – there is nothing necessarily mutually exclusive about these pairs of qualities. People actually do have all these qualities, but the patriarchal myth is that they don't, and at the moment the myth wins every time. In an androgynous society, each person would be able to express their own personal qualities in their own personal way, and not be expected to live up to some image of what they were supposed to be like.

But of course I was not alone in saying this. Five years earlier one of the better books on men (Fasteau, 1975) was saying things like:

Human beings, in other words, are naturally androgynous. This integration of the 'masculine' and 'feminine' aspects of the self is possible because opposition between them, sometimes characterized as 'doing versus being' or 'instrumental versus expressive' is false.

And two years before that such an eminent feminist as Mary Daly (1973) had been saying a whole series of things like this:

The healing process demands a reaching out toward completeness of human being in the members of both sexes – that is, movement toward androgynous being.

One of the most seductive and attractive versions of this doctrine was put forward by Sukie Colegrave (1979) in a book about the Chinese idea of the Yin and the Yang – the everlasting Tao (or Dao, as we say nowadays). After going into the whole question of the relationship between the Qian and the Kun, the Yin and the Yang, the masculine and the feminine, she says:

Obviously androgyny remains a very distant ideal. . . . [It is achieved] by the recognition that at every level of human nature, spiritual, psychological and physical, both sexual poles are present even though their relationship may be one-sided.

Her attempt to unite Daoism with Jung is something which Jung (1972) had already presaged with his great interest in Eastern philosophy and alchemy.

The message seems clear, then. Certain qualities (which we used to call feminine) are Yin qualities, which are culturally associated with women, but can be found in both women and men. Similarly, certain contrasting qualities (which we used to call masculine) are Yang qualities, which are often attributed socially to men, but can be found in women too. All that is wrong is that these two sets of qualities have become too separated and specialised. Each on its own is truncated, mutilated, inadequate to the idea of a whole human being, a fully functioning person. If we could encourage men to develop their Yin qualities, and women to develop their Yang qualities, we would achieve a good psychologically balanced androgyny. This kind of androgyny means that people have a well-rounded character, with Yin and Yang qualities fully integrated.

Now in its original derivation, Yin is 'the cloudy' or 'the overcast', and Yang is 'banners waving in the sun', and hence anything shone upon or bright. Soon the terms came to mean the shaded side of a hill, and the bright, sunlit side of it. The Shuo Kua (in Baynes, 1968) says:

> In ancient times the holy sages ... determined the tao of heaven and called it the dark and the light. They determined the tao of the earth and called it the yielding and the firm. They determined the tao of humanity and called it love and rectitude.

It can be seen that at this early date there was nothing about the feminine and the masculine – this was a later addition and interpretation. Nor is it true that Yin and Yang have a fixed connotation, applying to women and men alike. A Yin man is very different from a Yin woman; and a Yang woman is very different from a Yang man. This is such an obvious point that it hardly seems to need saying; yet it throws considerable doubt on the whole enterprise.

No doubt one of the things which often happens in therapy is that men get more in touch with their feelings, including grief and hurt, fear and guilt, and hence become more like women; just as women get more in touch with their power of self-determination and independence, and with feelings of anger and resentment, strength and determination, and hence more like men. But none of this affects the patriarchal system – it is more a difference of style than of structure.

It may well be true, as Sandra Bem (1977) and others have found, that people who possess both strong 'masculine' characteristics and strong 'feminine' characteristics are mentally healthier than people who are more one-sided and stereotyped, but this too does not make any difference to the patriarchal structure of our society.

And so it does not surprise me too much when I find a highly conservative textbook of psychology (Harari and Kaplan, 1977) advocating psychological androgyny (by which they mean not identifying exclusively with either the male or the female sex-role stereotype) and saying – 'Striving for androgyny is not a simple solution, but we feel it is a good one.' It will make you more popular, they say, and more well-adjusted.

Androgynous people are probably nicer and more effective than gender-stereotyped people, and in a non-patriarchal society it would be easier for people to be androgynous, but it seems clearer and clearer to me that in itself it means very little on a social scale. Joan Baez once said, 'I remember the first thought I ever had about women's lib was that if women could teach the men to cry, maybe we wouldn't have to go to war.' I don't know how she feels now about that statement, but what I believe is that men can cry and cry, and still pull the trigger; can tremble with fear and still drop the bomb; can go into paroxysms of guilt and still push the button. Just as women can be strong and fearless, and still let a man walk all over them.

There seems to be no evidence that men can get so Yin and women so Yang that they meet somehow in the middle. There are a few men about who can be mistaken for women, just as there are a few women about who can be mistaken for men, but this is not a trend, it is just a few exceptions. In any case, this seems, as an ideal, suspiciously close to the 1960s idea of unisex, which I think was always an illusion. Men didn't cease to be oppressive just by wearing pink shirts, long hair and flowered ties, any more than women ceased to be oppressed just by wearing jeans, short hair and T-shirts.

## Masculine and feminine

And this leads me to wonder whether there really are any 'eternally valid masculine and feminine qualities, underlying all the cultural overlays' as Singer (1976) seems to think. Certainly the Jungians think there are: both von Franz (1964) and Whitmont (1983) have long discussions of the feminine, the *anima,* which can be found in both women and men. Esther Harding (1971) sees the feminine qualities as 'emotion and relatedness' which are personal in character, and the masculine qualities as 'thinking, impersonality and spirit, leading to a concern for justice, and a cause'. Certainly Charlotte Bach thought there was – she used to talk of the feminine as 'the steamroller' and the masculine as 'the racing car'. Many spiritual traditions see the feminine as 'passive' and the male as 'active'.

What is much more well-established empirically, of course, is the set of characteristics found to be associated with males in our culture. The research shows that a whole set of qualities are expected of boys and men. As Broverman *et al.* (1970) have demonstrated, they include such things as:

| | |
|---|---|
| aggressive | not easily influenced |
| dominant | acts as a leader |
| competitive | self-confident |

These are the masculine qualities, and in the quite separate and distinct work of Bem (1974) the masculine qualities were again found to include:

| | |
|---|---|
| aggressive | acts like a leader |
| dominant | willing to take a stand |
| competitive | strong personality |

It seems clear that the stereotype is well fixed and well known. Duberman (1975), in her well researched book, finds that:

> The male ideal exalts being a good talker rather than a good listener, logic as opposed to emotion, conflict and adventure rather than constructive and incremental growth, self-confidence rather than humility and modesty, quick decision-making rather than thoughtful pondering, charisma and dynamism rather than a general desire to achieve even if power does not accompany the achievement, politics or business as an end in itself rather than a human concern as an end, a tough aggressive approach instead of a soft persuasive approach, responsiveness to external rewards (money, trophies, votes) rather than internal satisfaction, sexuality rather than sensuality.

Perhaps the fullest list of this kind, again based on a good deal of research, is from Warren Farrell (1975), who puts it this way:

> When I refer to something as 'masculine' or 'feminine' I am referring to the socialization of men or women as it exists, which is impossible to outline here. At an early age boys see models of men who seek material success, physical and psychological strength, leadership, invulnerability; who suppress their fear, control their emotions; who are pragmatic, know all the answers, never seek help, are tough and independent; who have a substantial degree of power, ambition, and physical and sexual aggression; who have control in sexual relations and in all relations, initiate sexual

relations, can get what they want when they want it; who generally want to be on top, be a protector, earn more than – and in general be better than – (preferably a man; if not, then a woman).... The woman's socialization encourages domesticity, nurturance, dependency, modesty, coyness, deviousness, warmth, emotionality, illogicality, the ability to be sensually and sexually arousing (while simultaneously properly inhibited and submissive), fearfulness, the need for protection, tenderness, fragility, displays of affection and 'sugar and spice and all things nice' (meaning: something extra to be added to the real substance). These traits are off-limits for the male.

In all this what is being said is not that these are the characteristics which all men have or are forbidden, or even some men have and are forbidden; what is being said is that these are the things which men get points for (or against) when their masculinity is being judged, either by themselves or others.

And it is definitely these characteristics which come up over and over again in the discussions in men's groups. The move toward androgyny is seen as a move toward accepting more of the qualities regarded as feminine (losing the horror of them which boys are expected to have) and questioning the qualities regarded as masculine. Often this was done in quite a sophisticated way. Here is a good proponent of men's groups speaking:

If I can define [femininity] at all, it means perhaps a lack of a harshness we tolerate in ourselves; there is a gentleness that seems to go more often with being female and that we call 'femininity' even though we would never dream of applying the same word to precisely the same gentleness when we find it in another man. A man who displays some of what we call femininity we might call gentle. A man who displays what the Dear Abbys mean by femininity we would call effeminate. [Marine, 1972]

This implies that men have a choice. They can choose to go along with the cultural expectations, or they can question them. And they can question them moderately, as Marine does, or radically, as Stoltenberg or the effeminists do. Any of this is possible because stereotyped masculinity is a defensive project. As Ryan (1985) puts it:

> Masculinity, then, can be viewed as a defensive construction developed over the early years out of a need to emphasise a difference, a separateness from the mother. In the extreme this is manifested by machismo behaviour with its emphasis on competitiveness, strength, aggressiveness, contempt for women and emotional shallowness, all serving to keep the male secure in his separate identity.

So if we take away the defences, and allow the feminine to come in, what happens?

It seems to me that because of the prevalence of patriarchy, and because of its all-pervasive influence (even extending into areas like the Tarot and astrology) we really have no idea of what males are really like under all the conditioning, or females either. Over the past few years, feminists have been struggling and wrestling with language and culture to try and discover what being a female might be – some of the bravest and most exciting efforts in this direction being by Mary Daly (1979, 1984). And it is worth noticing that in her striking book *Gyn/Ecology* she says:

> Experience proved that this word [androgyny] which we now recognise as expressing pseudo wholeness in its combination of distorted gender descriptions, failed and betrayed our thought.

This is the key to understanding why the usual idea of androgyny won't do. It is an attempt to repair the distortions of one patriarchal position by using material from the opposite distortion of another. But two blacks, as the old proverb has it, don't make a white. Or, you can't make a silk purse out of a sow's ear. Carol Christ (1980) put it this way in her discussion of the later work of the poet Adrienne Rich (1978):

Because she identifies men with the violence of their world, Rich declares:

There are words I cannot choose again:
*humanism   androgyny*
Such words have no shame in them, no diffidence
before the raging stoic grandmothers.

Androgyny implies that women accept what men have been as part of the wholeness they seek. This Rich can no longer accept. Increasingly, Rich sees more to admire in the resilient creative energy of women than in the union of or transcendence of male and female.

It is women who have seen this quicker than men, because men have gone along with the delusion that women are somehow more OK than men. But under patriarchy women's life and consciousness is distorted just as much as the life and consciousness of men is distorted. And so it is women who have seen through androgyny sooner than men, as for example Goldenberg (1979) when she says:

The androgyne is often invoked by people who want to deny the problems and anguish women in this society must face. I saw a classic example of this two years ago at a nationwide conference on Jungian psychology. A well-known woman who has written about androgyny was introduced by a younger woman student. The student told the audience how happy she was to welcome such a great woman to her campus. When the psychologist took the microphone, she admonished the student for referring to her as a woman, since she felt she was 'beyond that now'. During my presentation I remarked that the psychologist still looked like a woman to me.

Goldenberg goes on to point out how the androgyne tends to be a Utopian symbol, always to do with some distant future state, always at the end of things. It always retains, she says, 'an unrealistic, otherworldly quality'. It may be useful in opening up alternative ways of thinking, but ultimately it is a dead end.

Once we get to this point, it is easy to see that the usual concept of androgyny will not do at all.

> There is a paradox inherent in the ideal of androgyny, namely that, while it calls for the elimination of the sexual stereotyping of human virtues, it is itself formulated in terms of the discredited concepts of masculinity and femininity which it ultimately rejects. (Warren, 1980)

Further, the usual concept of androgyny does not even do justice to both sides of its equation, even on its own terms. As Gloria Steinem (1984) points out:

> *Androgyny* also raised the hope that female and male cultures could be perfectly blended in the ideal person; yet because the female side of the equation has yet to be affirmed, *androgyny* usually tilted toward the male. As a concept, it also raised anxiety levels by conjuring up a conformist, unisex vision, the very opposite of the individuality and uniqueness that feminism actually has in mind. (p. 158)

But if we accept that what people usually mean by androgyny is subject to all these flaws, is it possible still to maintain that there is a deeper version of androgyny which could still be valuable? Could we envisage a much more defensible notion of androgyny, soundly based on polarities of male and female which go down into the bedrock of archetypal experience, way below the distortions of everyday conscious social reality? All I can say is that, tempting as this idea is to me, I have not come across one statement of this idea which convinces me that the author has really gone beyond patriarchal definitions and prejudices.

So I now want to say that masculinity and femininity are fatally flawed concepts, culturally loaded, patriarchally based, unusable except as names of harmful stereotypes. Male and female are more biological terms, which bear no definite cultural meanings other than those we build, discover, choose, co-create and explore. And Yin and Yang are potentially misleading terms which really have nothing much to do with any of these four concepts: just a way of avoiding all the real and painful difficulties of redefining ourselves against the grain.

In doing this, I have found one enormous clue to be more helpful than any other. And as we resume our narrative, this is what we must now consider.

# CHAPTER 6

# Third channel of healing: 1

So far we have looked at two basic ways in which men can respond to the feminist message. (Of course there is another way: to retreat to a defensive position which simply pushes feminism away and tries to pretend that it doesn't exist, or is not important, or is incorrect.)

We have heard now how men can respond on a conscious level by changing laws and rules, and by changing our behaviour. We have found how men can respond on an unconscious level by doing counselling and therapy and discovering the roots of our oppressiveness. We have touched on the inadequacies of androgyny as a solution to any of the problems.

But in my own experience I came across a third way in which I could work, and this was the most valuable of all, though I think the others had to precede it. This was the discovery of the Great Goddess. It was also the most difficult of all.

### The Great Goddess

In 1978 I had separated from my wife, and taken up a new and much more intimate relationship than I had ever had before. And in the Spring of 1981 I started to enter into a new understanding that I was a spiritual being. This for me was a process rather like the feeling I had when I admitted that I was in love with Susie. It was a sort of crossing-the-Rubicon, risk-taking, boat-burning sort of feeling. Do I dare admit that I am a spiritual being? What are the implications? What was I letting myself in for?

It all happened very fast. I was obsessed with a search for what I needed, and I went through people, schools, literature with enormous speed and intensity. Eventually, in December, I arrived.

The thing happened when I came across a book called *The Spiral Dance: A Rebirth of the Ancient Religion of the Great Goddess* by Starhawk. I felt a shock of recognition that almost knocked me over.

Starhawk (1979) describes herself as a feminist witch, and not only studies the ancient archetypes, but actually lives them out in rituals and ceremonies. And in these observances, in mixed covens, there is a place for the male.

It needs to be said, because of the widespread ignorance about all this stuff, that the type of witchcraft we are talking about here is a Western tradition, usually called Wicca. This is a pagan form of worship, centring on a Goddess, who can take many forms, but at least the three persons known as the Maid, the Mother and the Hag (McLean, 1983), corresponding to the waxing, the full and the waning moon.

It reminded me of Keith Paton, who had been so impressed by the whole story about the Goddess that he had changed his name to Keith Motherson. Monica Sjöö, a very strong feminist artist and writer, had influenced him considerably, and in 1975 she had brought out a duplicated pamphlet called *The Ancient Religion of the Great Cosmic Mother of All*. In this work she had brought out the importance of the Goddess for feminists:

> Felt as if I was living in a hostile, alien culture which was trying to destroy me as a person. Wherever I looked around me, I could find NO positive, creative, strong women traditions or persons to identify with, and all the imagery I saw of women in art and all the media were a put-down of women.... Then the only images of strong women I could find at all were certain sculptures from very ancient Greece.

I found an image of the Theban Sphinx (1500 BC) – an extraordinary strange figure that is half lion, half bird (vulture?) with a woman's head. The expression of the woman's head is almost fearful and there is nothing at all sensuous or sexual about the image – one always reads about the ancient Goddess as a Fertility God.

At the time, I had not taken much notice of this, because it seemed to be all about women; useful for them, no doubt, but not much use to me. But by the time I had come to my insight about the Goddess being essential to men, too, Monica Sjöö (1981) had brought out a much improved, properly printed, well illustrated version of her earlier pamphlet. What did she, as a Goddess-identified woman, have to say about the male?

> *When the Goddess begets a son,* and he becomes the Moon-Hero and the newborn Spirit of the Vegetation (the Green Child) – the origin of all the dying and resurrecting male gods – She, like Ishtar of Babylon, goes to the Underworld to save him. . . . She arrives in the ultimate Place of Death naked and weakened, and undergoes Herself a terrible kind of spiritual-psychic death in order to restore the world. . . .
>
> *She Herself kills Her son Tammuz,* in Her form of wild strength, the She-Bear or She-Boar. Then as Ishtar She mourns Tammuz on the 'Fast of Lamentation' or Ramadan. Rites of Tammuz-Attis-Adonis-Dionysus were always attended by wailing, mourning women, smeared with ashes and head-shorn. Ishtar ultimately finds and restores Her son – later Her lover – to rebirth and immortality. . . . In Egyptian mythology, it is Isis, the original Great Mother, who goes over the Earth seeking Her sacrificed brother/lover Osiris. The immortal Goddess finds and pieces together the severed parts of his body, renewing the world. Osiris was her Moon-Fruit, the vegetation that was yearly destroyed and then regenerated by Her.

Here again, in this deep and lengthy study of the Goddess, there is a place for the male, so long as he depends on the Goddess and recognises her authority and power. But again he has to be prepared to die.

As I ranged further over the literature of the Goddess, I found that she had indeed been inspiring to feminists, and in a directly political way. More than one chapter in the excellent McAllister (1982) bears this out, and in the same year Charlene Spretnak (1982) edited a whole book called *The Politics of Women's Spirituality,* with chapters by Merlin Stone, Marija Gimbutas, Adrienne Rich, Starhawk, Carol Christ, Robin Morgan, Phyllis Chesler, Gloria Steinem, Margot Adler, Judy Chicago, Sally Gearhart, Mary Daly, Naomi Goldenberg, Marge Piercy, Emily Culpepper, Chellis Glendinning and many others.

These people made it clear, over and over again, that the basic idea of the Goddess is a necessary one if we are to question patriarchy at the deepest and most serious level. Listen to Carol Christ telling it:

> Because religion has such a compelling hold on the deep
> psyches of so many people, feminists cannot afford to leave
> it in the hands of the fathers. Even people who no longer
> 'believe in God' or participate in the institutional structure
> of patriarchal religion still may not be free of the power of
> the symbolism of God the Father. A symbol's effect does not
> depend on rational assent, for a symbol also functions on
> levels of the psyche other than the rational. Religion fulfils
> deep psychic needs by providing symbols and rituals that
> enable people to cope with limit situations in human life
> (death, evil, suffering) and to pass through life's important
> transitions (birth, sexuality, death). Even people who consider
> themselves completely secularized will often find themselves
> sitting in a church or synagogue when a friend or relative
> gets married, or when a parent or friend has died. The
> symbols associated with these important rituals cannot fail
> to affect the deep or unconscious structures of the mind of
> even a person who has rejected these symbolisms on a

conscious level – especially if the person is under stress. The reason for the continuing effect of religious symbols is that the mind abhors a vacuum. Symbol systems cannot simply be rejected, they must be replaced. Where there is not any replacement, the mind will revert to familiar structures at times of crisis, bafflement or defeat.

This is a crucial point, which really forms the whole basis of the argument in the book I am writing here. We don't just live in a conscious world, where everything is clear, and out there, and on the surface. We also live in the world of the unconscious, where fantasy reigns, and where what is important is something deep inside us. All the time we are apparently attending to business, to marriage, to sport, to gardening, we are secretly operating under the influence of our guiding fictions.

In the case of the Goddess, I felt inspired to tune in deliberately to the energies which Monica Sjöö and Starhawk had spoken of. One result was this poem:

IN THE WOOD

This is the place.
In the circle of trees I sit down.
It is early. I listen. It starts.
Moving down
Moving down to the centre
The dark
The lovely fearsome nourishing darkness
Down there
Into Her realm. Into Her space. Into Her time.
Down, down to infinity.
Deeper, deeper into the dark realm
All the way, nothing held back, here I go.
And then She comes
And then She is there
I feel the thrill touching my heart
Opening it up, filling it to bursting, singing in it

My heart, Her heart now, singing, wide open, all full
All full of Her
Her darkness, Her blood, Her power, Her changes,
Her force, Her awe, Her strength, Her depth,
Her infinite love, Her wisdom, Her ugliness/beauty
All filling me now.

It can be seen from this poem that I felt very inspired by the Goddess. And because I had learned about her from feminist women, it was not a male and flattering image of the Goddess that I had, but a strong female vision of the Goddess:

> The Great Cosmic Mountain Mother, who was the Mother of the Wild Animals – who was the Dark ocean, and the Night and Day Sky – begets the Silver Egg, or fruit of Her Night Sky, the Moon. She is *both* Moon and the Earth. And the ancient Bird and Snake Goddess of Sky and Air begets a daughter – the pregnant Earth, Goddess of Vegetation. *Both Mother and Daughter are linked with the Moon. The Moon, as daughter of the Great Mother, is known as the Triple Goddess.* She presides over *all* acts of generation, whether physical, spiritual or intellectual. Her triple aspect expresses the three phases of the Moon: Waxing (renewal), Full (rebirth) and Waning (periodic death). She is, as the New or Waxing Moon, the White Goddess of birth and growth. She is, as the Full Moon, the Red Goddess of love and battle. She is, as the Old or Waning Moon, the Black Goddess of death and divination. These are the *Three phases of a woman's life, all natural and all magical.* Transience and Immortality are different aspects of the Goddess. The Moon as the daughter-fruit of the Great Mother's Sky expresses the essential unity of Her Cosmos. Moon and Sun are the eyes of the Heavenly Mother, the all-seeing One. We still talk of 'heavenly bodies' and of stars 'looking down on us'. (Sjöö and Mor, 1981)

But the Great Goddess is also, and very importantly, an underworld goddess. Down there in the darkness – for the

Goddess was usually approached through caves – the miracles of birth and creativity were honoured and adored. Then most sacred ceremonies of death and rebirth took place down there in the depths. At the entrance to the cave there was a maze, presided over by a mythical woman. The initiate had to find the way through the underworld – the Mother – going through symbolic death to be reborn again through her on a deeper psychic level.

> Simultaneously, by dancing the winding and unwinding Spiral, the initiate reached back to the *Still Heart of the Cosmos,* and so immortality, through Her. (Sjöö and Mor, 1981)

Once we see the richness and value of the downward path, accepting that what is down there can be positive, everything changes. We lose our fear, carefully instilled by the patriarchy, of what is underneath, behind and below. The vortex becomes positive, the blood becomes positive, the darkness and silence become positive. A great deal of material has been coming out recently about the Great Goddess, challenging and revising many of our old assumptions. For example, look at Barbara Walker's (1983) article on Kali Ma, where she presents material like this:

> Kali was the basic archetypal image of the birth-and-death Mother, simultaneously womb and tomb, giver of life and devourer of her children: the same image portrayed in a thousand ancient religions. . . . As a Mother, Kali was called Treasure-House of Compassion (karuna), Giver of Life to the world, the Life of all lives. Contrary to the West's idea of her as a purely destructive Goddess, she was the fount of every kind of love, which flowed into the world only through her agents on earth, women. Thus it was said that a male worshipper of Kali 'bows down at the feet of women', regarding them as his rightful teachers.

The entry goes on for six pages, and includes this quotation from the Nirvana Tantra:

> Compared with the vast sea of the being of Kali, the existence
> of Brahma and the other gods is nothing but such a little
> water as is contained in the hollow made by a cow's hoof.
> Just as it is impossible for a hollow made by a cow's hoof
> to form a notion of the unfathomable depths of a sea, so it
> is impossible for Brahma and other gods to have a knowledge
> of the nature of Kali.

More soberly, Ken Wilber (1981) makes an important distinction between the Great Mother and the Great Goddess. He outlines various levels of development in anthropological terms, and links the Great Mother with level 3 (magical sacrifices for fertility and so on) but the Great Goddess with level 6 (self-sacrifice in awareness, openness to archetypal symbols and so on). In other words, the Great Mother is very closely tied in to a pre-personal and tribal stage of development, while the Great Goddess is to do with a transpersonal stage of very high development. It is very easy, he says, to confuse the two, but it is also important not to, because if we do, we may dismiss the sophistication of the Great Goddess by treating her as if she were simply and primitively the Great Mother.

> There should be no confusion as to how Great Mother
> religion and Great Goddess religion could exist side by side,
> often in the same place, at the same time, and frequently
> using the same symbols. For this is simply the phenomenon
> of exoteric and esoteric religion in general. That is, from
> almost the beginning of mankind's religious expressions,
> those expressions have been understood exoterically or
> outwardly, and esoterically or inwardly. Every great world
> religion, in fact, has *both* exoteric and esoteric aspects, and
> those aspects usually coexist perfectly with one another, the
> exoteric rituals serving the masses, the esoteric serving the
> advanced. All I am doing is applying this perennial

distinction to the mythic-membership religions of the Mother Goddess – in each instance, are they exoteric, of the Great Mother, or esoteric, of the Great Goddess? (Wilber, 1981)

Göttner-Abendroth (1985) clarifies matters even more by distinguishing between three periods of mythology, which she calls the *rural matriarchal*, the *urban matriarchal* and the *cyclic battle of the demons*. The relationship we are interested in between a powerful Goddess and a supportive Horned God belongs to the urban matriarchal period, where we have such pairs as Isis and Osiris, Inanna and Dumuzi, Cybele and Attis, and Demeter and Dionysus. This represents the peak of Goddess spirituality, before the change into the cyclic battle of the demons and the subsequent incursion of the patriarchal religions.

In order to discover more about what this really meant, I joined a Moon group, organised along Wiccan lines, but not actually calling itself that. We celebrated the full moons and the eight great festivals of Imbolc, Spring Equinox, Beltane, Midsummer, Lughnasad, Autumn Equinox, Samhain and Yule. From this I learnt a great deal, both about the Goddess and about the Horned God.

It needs to be said that there is some doubt as to the continuity of the Wiccan tradition. As with many other esoteric traditions, there are enormous unexplained gaps. So although witchcraft claims to go back to neolithic times, and to be connected with the witches of previous centuries, most of the ceremonies now in existence seem to have their origins in the work of Gerald Gardner (1954, 1959) and Doreen Valiente (1978). Alex and Maxine Sanders (see Farrar and Farrar, 1984) were also influential in starting a number of covens with quite an emphasis on order and discipline, though this was sometimes not kept to too well, as Adler (1979) remarks. In fact, Adler has the best discussion that I have seen of this whole matter, and eventually seems to come to the conclusion that the exact details of the continuity of the tradition do not matter too much. The basic alchemy, if we can put it that way, resides in the attitude that one has when practising the ceremonies:

The lack of dogma in the Craft, the fact that one can *worship* the Goddess without *believing* in Her, that one can accept the Goddess as 'Muse' and the Craft as a form of ancient knowledge to be tested by experience – these are precisely the things that have caused the Craft to survive, to revive, and to be re-created in this century.

The Craft in general has a fairly fixed set of symbols. The Goddess is the Moon in her three aspects or phases. The Horned God is most often pictured as lord of animals, lord of the hunt, lord of death and what lies beyond. The four elements are important – earth, air, fire and water – and the four directions – North, East, South and West – and the four tools – Pentacle, Athame, Wand and Cup. The four festivals – Imbolc, Beltane, Lughnasad and Samhain – are very important, and the other four, which have more to do with the Sun, are important too – Spring Equinox, Midsummer, Autumn Equinox and Midwinter.

Some of this is similar to ritual magic, but this is rather a different tradition: for example, in ritual magic the purpose of the circle is to keep out dangerous spirits which have been conjured up for the magician's safety, while in witchcraft the purpose of the circle is to contain and concentrate the energies raised. Another distinction is emphasised by Leo Martello, a modern witch, who says:

> Witchcraft is a pre-Christian faith. . . . It tends to be matriarchal whereas both Christianity and Satanism are patriarchal and male chauvinist. The latter two are merely opposite sides of the same coin. Witchcraft, as the Old Religion, is a coin of a different vintage, predating both. (Quoted in Walker, 1983)

But what kind of religion is it really? We have already dropped some hints that it is not a religion on the model of Christianity, Islam or Judaism, where there are strict dogmas which have to be believed, and a central theology which is held to very strictly.

Perhaps the best account I have seen of the approach comes from a recent book by Matthews and Matthews (1985):

> God and initiate are co-creators, each reflecting the worlds in which they live. . . . By identification and subsequent affiliation with the god, the initiate works with certain energies which are themselves transformative. By close attention and sensitivity to the energies represented by the god-form, the initiate is drawn into intimate contact with and awareness of that archetypal energy. This is what is meant when we speak of someone 'being contacted'. It forms the basis of religion when it is informed by cosmic understanding rather than naive superstition. In this way, it is possible to work with pagan god-forms (relating as they are to energies now represented by later archetypes), as long as their energies are fully synthesized into modern consciousness.

This ties in very well with the view of Ken Wilber, which we have already seen, that the Great Goddess can be related to on an archetypal level, in what he calls the subtle stage of psychospiritual development.

If this is so, then we may look to see in the future a better-developed thealogy of the Great Goddess, which says much more about the exact spiritual position being adopted here. One of the people who is trying to do this work is Rosemary Radford Ruether (1983), who has much to say about the way in which religion can either support sexism or diminish it. Until we do better justice on a spiritual level to the female, she says, sexism will flourish.

At a personal level, this was all very new and very challenging. I felt very unsure of myself at first, because I had always steered clear of anything that sounded like the occult or the magical, rather looking down on it all as the almost pathological desire to get power in an eccentric and possibly dangerous way. But some of the people I was meeting and reading seemed to have their feet on the ground and to be very whole people, politically active and sound. The best of them were relying on their own experience in just the way that the best people I had met in the growth movement went by their own experience, not taking things on trust, but living them out in their own lives. One book which I found very helpful in the early days of my search was Robinson's *Living the Questions* (1978), and this phrase rang very true for me. I was living my questions, not just thinking about them. I remember one vision I had was of Susie and I as two very ancient blocks of stone with jagged edges, which when brought together fitted with a very satisfying sound, and fused into one. And a few months later, I heard her answering a question about the Goddess in such a way that her own deep appreciation of the Goddess, quite different from mine but compatible with it, came out to my delighted surprise, because I had never asked her about it.

So finding the Goddess was also like coming home. It was like something being restored which had been there before, and had been taken away. It was like finding a long-lost mother. There was this combination of strangeness and familiarity about it. I went around noticing so many things I hadn't noticed before – for example, in Athena one day I had the usual reactions to the way women were pictured – sexually objectified, turned into objects for men's use, seen through men's eyes, prettified, falsified, all that familiar stuff – and then I realised it could be looked at quite differently. I could see it as the Goddess insisting on being recognised – as if under all the falsification there was a power which could not be denied, and which would press on through, regardless of anyone's attempt to deny it. The very effort to twist it was testimony to the urgent need to do something, anything, about it. You couldn't just leave it alone. And this made me think again of the Virgin Mary, which is such a poor and inadequate image of the female. As Warner (1978) has pointed out, the Goddess continually peers out of the eyes of the Virgin Mary, because Mary is the only place to put the female energy in the framework of Christianity. So here again is testimony to the way in which the Goddess comes back despite all attempts to get rid of Her forever.

One of the things which feminists often say is that men suck off female energy and drain it – that they are continually plugging in to female energy and using it, without ever acknowledging that this is the way in which they get whatever power they have. And it now began to strike me that this is absolutely true – except that if men can go directly to the Goddess and suck off Her, as it were, or plug in to Her, they won't need to put any kind of drain on individual women – in fact, they will be able to give more to the women in their lives. By acknowledging that they do really need that female power and strength, men can get it direct from the source, so to speak, and gain immensely from doing so, in such a way that the women around them can gain immensely, too. What we need to know is how exactly this can happen. So this raises the whole question of what now is to be the relationship between the female and the male. How can men relate to women better, given this kind of understanding?

And the same questions arise about children, too. Childcare is a key issue in the renewal of male consciousness, and there have been many articles on this in *Achilles Heel* and the *Men's Antisexist Newsletter*. The essential point is made by John Lennon in a TV interview which I saw:

It's been five years since I recorded. It could have been twenty. Life is long. I wanted to give Sean five years of being there all the time. There's a price to pay for giving attention to children. If I can't deal with a child, I can't deal with anything. No matter what artistic gains I may get, or how many gold records, if I can't make a success out of the relationship with people I supposedly love, then anything else is bullshit.

I don't know how I could say it any better than that. I think at the end of his life, John Lennon was understanding how to relate to a woman, and how to relate to a child, not only on a practical level, but also on a spiritual level. And it is time now to go to look at the male side of all this.

# CHAPTER 7

# Third channel of healing: 2

It is necessary to deal with the Goddess first, because She represents the image of female power which is necessary to turn us round completely. I believe that unless and until both men and women genuinely believe that the female can be powerful, men are going to hang on to their power. But conversely, if men can be convinced that the female is strong and can handle power, their panic at the idea of a power vacuum can be assuaged. But the question then arises – in a world where women have taken their power, what is the place for a man?

## The Horned God

The male figure compatible with the Goddess is the Horned God. And the image of the male which comes out of this archetypal figure is very different from any of the usual pictures of masculinity in our culture. Starhawk (1979) says:

> He is difficult to understand because He does not fit into any of the expected stereotypes, neither those of the 'macho' male nor the reverse-images of those who deliberately seek effeminacy. He is gentle, tender and comforting, but He is also the Hunter. He is the Dying God – but His death is always in the service of the life force. He is untamed sexuality – but sexuality as a deep, holy, connecting power.

He is the power of feeling, and the image of what men could be if they were liberated from the constraints of patriarchal culture.

Here is a declared feminist actually putting forward a vision of the male which she can accept and approve of. Here there is no sense that masculinity is something to be disposed of or set aside or replaced. Rather, it is something to be revalued and seen afresh, with new eyes. She went on to say:

For men, the God is the image of inner power and of a potency that is more than merely sexual. He is the undivided Self, in which mind is not split from body, nor spirit from flesh. United, both can function at the peak of creative and emotional power.

Here again was a new sort of encouragement. *The Undivided Self* was the title of a booklet I had edited two or three years previously, all about therapy and how the aim of humanistic therapy was to heal the splits of mind and body, intellect and feelings, left and right, and so forth. It was inspiring to find this now heralded as a spiritual vision of the male. Starhawk went on to say this:

The God embodies the power of feeling. His animal horns represent the truth of undisguised emotion, which seeks to please no masters. He is untamed. But untamed feelings are very different from enacted violence. The God is the life force, the life cycle. He remains within the orbit of the Goddess; his power is always directed toward the service of life.

Here was the key. The male was safe, positive, so long as it was in the service of the Goddess. The relationship with the Goddess was the guarantee that patriarchy would not return. But this relationship was not easy: it had to be won by an intense experience of humility and sacrifice. As Starhawk explained:

For both women and men, the God is also the Dying God. As such, He represents the giving over that sustains life: Death in the service of the life force. Life is characterised by many losses, and, unless the pain of each one is fully felt and worked through, it remains buried in the psyche, where, like a festering sore that never heals, it exudes emotional poison. The Dying God embodies the concept of loss. In rituals, as we enact his death over and over again, we release the emotions surrounding our own losses, lance the wounds, and win through to the healing promised by his rebirth. This psychological purging was the true purpose of dramatic tragedy, which originated in Greece out of the rites of the dying God Dionysus. . . . The God becomes the Comforter and Consoler of Hearts, who teaches us to understand death through his example. He embodies the warmth, tenderness and compassion that are the true complement of male aggression.

This now linked up with another strand of my own experience. Not only did it speak of many times when I felt this sort of thing in my own therapy, but it also related to the whole process of spiritual development which I had been involved in, and which had been illuminated by the work of Ken Wilber.

Wilber (1980) says that there is a definite path of psycho-spiritual development, and that all of us are somewhere on this path, whether we know it or not, and whether we like it or not. And movement along this path is a dialectical matter, where each step forward means contradicting the previous one, and leaving something cherished behind. It means dying to our old notion of who and what we are, and taking on a new notion, which each time is fuller and richer, but as time goes on begins to seem too small and too restricting. All of us are familiar with the earlier phases of this process: leaving the symbiosis of the womb for a separate body; leaving the separate body for a family identity; leaving the family identity for a peer identity; leaving the peer identity for a separate mental ego – each of these revisions of the self is well documented and widely experienced.

The next step on the path – leaving the mental ego for the real self – was something I had been familiar with for some years, and had written about at length (Rowan, 1976). It was one of the basic aims of humanistic therapy, and I had seen this change happening in myself and a number of other people. It represented a growth of authenticity which had been written about in great detail by many writers. This level is variously referred to as the 'integration of all lower levels' (Sullivan *et al.*, 1957), 'integrated' (Loevinger, 1976), 'self-actualising' (Maslow, 1968), 'autonomous' (Fromm, 1942; Riesman, 1954), 'with individual principles' (Kohlberg, 1969), 'growth oriented' (Alderfer, 1972), 'integrating persons' (Mahrer, 1978), 'the fully functioning person' (Rogers, 1961) and so on. Wilber called this the Centaur stage, and said:

> This integrated self, wherein mind and body are
> harmoniously one, we call the 'centaur'. The centaur: the
> great mythological being with animal body and human-mind
> existing in a perfect state of at-one-ment.

I have written at some length about this elsewhere (Rowan, 1983) so not too much needs to be said here. But the next step on the path is to leave the real self for the greater self – sometimes called the higher self, the deeper self, the transpersonal self, the subtle self, etc. This is something I had just begun to experience in my own life, and this stuff about the God made a lot of sense to me personally.

### Archetypes

At this stage we have to deal with the whole question of the symbols by which we live. We are surrounded by ideals and compulsions, as it were, which press on us from the culture in which we live. We are immersed in a sea of images of how we should be, of how we should live our lives, which present themselves as ideals for us to live up to. They are everywhere, and some of them have long histories, and can be incredibly ancient. For example, Hairy Chested Macho Man, an ideal of today, goes back to the heroes of ancient cultures, such as Hercules. Another ideal of today, the Dedicated White Coated Scientist, goes back to gods of wisdom and enlightenment such as Apollo.

The great psychologist Carl Jung taught us long ago that these ideals – or archetypes, as he called them more precisely – needed to be studied in their own right. What happens at an archetypal level affects everything we do. If the archetypes are healthy, we are healthy; if the archetypes crumble, our civilisation crumbles too.

And what is happening today is that a slow change at the level of the archetypes has affected all of us. Starting way back around the beginning of the nineteenth century, people have become more and more aware of a shift, a cracking, a slide in the underlying layers of the collective unconscious. From about 1800 it became more and more obvious that the overwhelming imbalance in favour of all that was masculine was being questioned.

It came out in the Romantic Movement, where what was natural started to be appreciated. It came out in the movement for girls' education. It came out in the creation of art and music schools. It came out in a new kind of cultivation of feelings and sensibility. It seemed that a new kind of balance was emerging at all levels, where the male and the female would both be valued and honoured. But then there came a long setback because of the very fast development of science and technology. The masculine imbalance returned, with added strength, and this has continued for many years. But now science and technology has overreached itself, and we have all become aware of the terrible consequences. The screaming devastation of Hiroshima, the dead lakes and dust-bowls of the USA, the killing of the forests, the selfish snatching of the earth's resources, all tell us that something must change.

And sure enough, at an archetypal level the old idols of masculinity are falling apart. The old male stereotypes cannot inspire us any more. We can't simply believe in Hairy Chested Macho Man, we can't believe in All Wise Daddy, we can't believe in the Dedicated White Coated Scientist, we can't believe in the Cheery Life and Soul of the Party, we can't believe in the White Haired Patriarch, we can't believe in the Romantic Bohemian Artist Struggling in a Garret, we can't believe in the Serious Responsible Worker with Nose to the Grindstone.

And the reason why we can't believe in them any more is because they have been shown up for what they are. The people who have done this showing up most effectively have been the women usually known as feminists. The curious thing is that many of them don't realise that they are working at an archetypal level at all. But the effect of what they are doing is to make these old ideals, these current idols, seem more and more like the inflated statues they are, put up to impress, but really now hollow and without substance. We can't fall down and worship a balloon.

But of course these women haven't just questioned these images in a cool and quiet way. They have been deeply indignant about the trick that has been played upon them – a whole civilisation based upon masculine ideals and masculine images, which systematically put down and oppressed all that was female.

Hairy Chested Macho Man can actually beat up women – a lot of male violence against women stems from this image – but more often just puts them down, belittles them and uses them. (Sometimes under the guise of putting them on a pedestal.) The All Wise Daddy depends on the rest of the family to be foolish so that he can be wise – making them small is somehow supposed to make him great. The Dedicated White Coated Scientist turns out to be mainly concerned with boosting his own ego and competing aggressively with the scientist next door, and is quite capable of producing weapons that will destroy humanity, ecological invasions that destroy nature, nuclear waste that will be a health hazard and a lure to terrorists for millennia, and a medical system more interested in new machines, new instruments and new drugs than it is in people. The Cheery Life and

Soul of the Party turns out to be an insensitive misogynist whose main interest is in his cock. The White Haired Patriarch turns out to be a banker sitting on the world's wealth and advising governments how to increase his profits. The Romantic Bohemian Artist Struggling in a Garret turns out to be someone who uses women as stepping stones to advancement, only using weakness as his ally rather than strength, as with the others. And the Serious Responsible Worker with Nose to the Grindstone turns out to be just as oppressive as any of the others, cutting himself off from emotions so that he can work more efficiently for more hours for more money for more things, none of which can compensate for failing to relate emotionally to women and children and other men in his world.

All these images, the feminists discovered painfully, are about oppressing women in some mode or other, and about restricting the female archetypes to just those acceptable to men as serving them in some fashion. They named the system as Patriarchy, and this helped them to see the parts of the system more clearly as all working together. But of course once a system gets seriously damaged in one of its parts, this can throw out the whole way in which it works. Once the phrase 'male chauvinist pig' gets into the language, so that even those who thoroughly disagree with it know what it means, a crack has appeared in the structure – a crack which continues to widen as time goes on.

When idols crumble in this way, we wonder what to do. The heroic way is of course to do without idols at all; but this sounds better in theory than it actually is in practice. Very few of us can really do without some kind of image of what we want to be like, of what we are aiming at. At a very deep level, as Jung pointed out long ago, we need some archetypal picture of what we may be, of what we can be. We need some sort of ideal to live up to – what Adler called a guiding fiction – something to make us feel that we are on the right track.

The male figure compatible with the Goddess is the Horned God. And the image of the male which comes out of this archetypal figure is very different from any of the usual pictures of masculinity in our culture. As Gary Lingen (1983) says:

The Horned One represents powerful positive male qualities which derive from deep natural sources within us rather than the stereotypes and violence and emotional crippling which has affected almost all the men and boys within our society.

For example, in our usual way of thinking, men are strong. This means being well-armoured and invulnerable. For a man to become vulnerable would mean to take off the armour and hence to be weak and feminine. It would have to be one or the other – either strong or vulnerable. But the Horned God is strong and vulnerable at the same time. He is not afraid to die because he knows he will be reborn. He is the Lord of Death and Rebirth.

Again, in our usual way of thinking, a man's mind has to be in charge of his body. If his body takes over, he becomes lazy, or hurtful, or lustful or gluttonous, and so the mind has to come in for discipline and control. But the Horned God is the Undivided Self, in which mind is not split from body, nor spirit from flesh. There is a wholeness there, which means that we can now act spontaneously and adequately at the same time.

The ordinary way of thinking holds that men are steady and dependable. Men should stick to one thing, and their word should be unchanging. But the Horned God is all about change. He is Lord of the Dance (see Figure 3), and together with the Goddess symbolises the spiral dance of life. He brings personal change and social change. He shows us the madness in the tasks of the sane world of every day. He presents us with a sense of being at the edges, the borderlines, so that we can't tell whether he is mad or sane, businessman or artist, bourgeois or revolutionary, poet or printer, wild or sober, sexual or psychic, conscious or unconscious.

And the standard way of thinking about men is to say that they must be continuously male. If they drop their masculinity even once, and become female even in one way, they are labelled feminine for ever, and never respected in the same way. But the Horned God has complete freedom in this respect. As a shape-

*Figure 3   Robin Goodfellow as Lord of the Dance: a medieval woodcut*

shifter, he can be male or female, essentially bisexual. As Lord of the Waters, he can go down into the collective unconscious and start to understand at a deep level what it is to menstruate, what it is to give birth, what it is to have a hole instead of a pole. Here he knows about durable weakness and unheroic strength (see Hillman, 1978).

These are concrete matters. They can be experienced in rituals where we get in touch with the powers of the Horned One. The faces of the god are found in personal experiences, and they say – 'Look at this. Feel this. Know this within yourself and name its power so that you can draw it forth.' This is the new paganism. As Gary Lingen says:

> The Horned One is a positive model for male power – free from the patriarchy and all other authoritarian models – as he grows and passes through his changes during the wheel of the year, he remains in relationship to and not separate from the prime life and nurturing force – the Goddess.

The rituals of Wicca include both the male and the female together.

Having got this much from books, it seemed that the next step was to get involved in some living experiences which would enable me to feel the truth or falsity of these ideas for myself. I joined a group which met at the full moon and at each of the eight great festivals of the pagan world. We did not call ourselves witches, but the group was clearly in the broad Wiccan tradition.

As Margot Adler (1979) has told us, there is now a huge variety of groups and practices concerned with the Goddess, but Wicca is one of the most prominent among them. Adler says:

> The deities of most Wicca groups are two: the God, lord of animals, lord of death and beyond, and the Goddess, the triple Goddess in her three aspects: Maiden, Mother and Crone. Each aspect is symbolized by a phase of the moon – the waxing crescent, the full moon and the waning crescent. In general, there is a great divergence among the Wicca as to what these 'gods' are. Are they thought forms, built up over centuries? Are they archetypes? Are they literal entities? The answer depends on whom you talk to.

For our present purposes it seems to make sense to think of the Horned God as an archetype. Like all archetypes, he can be focussed on and opened up to. He can enter into our minds and bodies, and fill us with a sense of the divine. And when this happens, we are more caring about the Earth.

Politically I think this is one of the most important aspects of the Horned God for men. Starhawk (1982) emphasised the very direct link between Goddess worship and the anti-nuclear campaign:

> For a man, the personal relationship with Gaea is a way out of the cultural trap, because a man who embraces his own connection with the Goddess experiences the power of nurturing within himself, independent of his tie to a living woman. Just as, once the ground has been named, a woman can no longer remain completely merged with it, so, too, a man, once the ground has been named as a living reality, can no longer remain so comfortably split from it. Gaea makes the power of the mother a conscious force, something with which we must come to terms.

We cannot experience the Earth as our Mother Goddess and let her be poisoned by plutonium.

Similarly, we cannot feel the Horned God within us as the spirit of the trees, the animals, and let all that be destroyed by acid rain or nuclear war. It is no accident that the women of Greenham Common have taken and used the Goddess symbols – the snake, the spider's web, the bird, the labyrinth – in their powerful and sustained protest against cruise missiles.

Equally political is the inability of those who love the Goddess to oppress women. Starhawk asks groups to whom she speaks – 'Would you like to have a vision of the Goddess?' When they indicate that the answer is yes, she tells them to turn and look at the person sitting next to them. The Goddess is immanent, not abstract. If every woman is the Goddess, then every woman is to be respected and genuinely met. This is a real alternative to male chauvinism.

### Some implications

From the position we have now reached, we can begin to sketch in some ways in which the requirements of feminism can be fulfilled.

## Male privilege

As we move out of the patriarchal period, there is bound to be some very uncomfortable adjustment to be made, both for women and for men. But if we can be aware of each other's problems in this transition, the pain can be minimised. Men will need to give much more emotional support to women than they have done in the past, learning how to be 'wives' and 'midwives' to the emergence of strong, Goddess-identified women who look to other women for most of their guidance. Women will have to learn how to confront men without alienating them, pushing them to change and to learn from other men while respecting their maleness. Starhawk (1982) is good on this issue:

> By *maleness*, I do not mean any of the qualities that have been arbitrarily assigned to men as if they didn't apply to women. I do not mean such things as aggression, assertion, activity, yang-ness, rationality and logos. I mean only the power of being at home – strong, potent and awake to feeling in a male body.

There is nothing necessarily oppressive about this kind of maleness. In the present set-up, being male carries with it certain privileges, and in the transition period all we can do is to be aware of this, and to question our own need for such privileges. Most of them are actually of dubious advantage when looked at critically and freshly, as we saw in Chapter 3.

## Machismo

This is defined in the dictionary as 'an exaggerated sense of masculinity stressing such attributes as physical courage, virility, domination of women and aggressiveness or violence.' It always brings with it a great fear of being shown up as in any way not being 'a real man'. It is this fear which gives us the clue to how unreal and precarious it always is. Goldberg (1980) gives six features of the macho orientation:

1   Strongly 'rational' or problem-solving, the problem being narrowly defined and isolated.

2   Threatened by weakness, fear, vulnerability or any
    suggestion that he can't solve problems by himself.
3   Competitive toward other men, and compulsively
    needing to prove himself superior and able to control
    and dominate situations while projecting an image of
    self-containment and strength. 'Stay cool and get ahead.'
4   Impatient and suspicious of any process which has no
    clear-cut path or timetable and promises no specific
    results.
5   Needing to project a totally masculine image while
    defensively denying anything in him that might be
    construed as feminine, effeminate or homosexual.
6   Fearful of depending on and trusting someone else.

I have slightly altered Goldberg's wording, because he is very
unaware of some of the implications of what he is saying.
Indeed, to use the word 'machismo' or 'macho' at all can in
itself be unaware, because as Tapia (1979) has said:

> Machismo is not in itself a cultural ethic for Latinos, but
> more so a product of imperialism and colonialism....
> Machismo is an act of overt power over Latinas and less
> macho or effeminate men, but it is power coming from
> powerlessness.... The more politically conscious Latino men
> become, the more we will be able to see that machismo is
> our trade-off for a false sense of power, a trade-off for a
> history of genocide and class oppression.

So we need to be quite cautious in using such a word at all, even
though it does have a certain ring to it which invented words
often lack. Miller and Swift (1979) have a good discussion of
some of these points.

Again all this became very personal for me. Susie and I were
doing workshops on sexuality and sex roles, and over and over
again we found that these new insights about the Goddess and
the Horned God made our work both easier and deeper. Instead

of a sort of underlying despair about the possibility of women and men relating together in our society, there was a sort of underlying hope.

But there was also much more appreciation that heterosexuality did not have to be the answer to everything. Once I began to appreciate that being a male was OK, that meant that the male body was OK, and that meant that male bodies could be beautiful, attractive, exciting. The whole world of bisexuality and homosexuality opened up.

And I found that, just as many of the women who loved the Goddess were lesbian, many of the followers of the Horned God were gay. In America, one of the groups was called the Radical Faeries, politically active gay men who are spiritually in the pagan tradition. There are several all-male groups, such as the Kathexis Anthropos Coven in New York State, Anubis in Maine, the Minoan Brotherhood in Florida and so on. I don't know of any in Britain, and it seems that on both sides of the Atlantic there is some homophobia in Craft and magical circles. Adler (1979) has a good deal to say about Dianic and other all-female covens, but nothing at all to say about all-male equivalents. The Farrars (1984) do mention all-male covens, but only to warn against them. A gay man in New York wrote to me to say that he had found a disappointing amount of homophobia amongst pagans in his area.

Gary Lingen (1985) is much more aware of the issues raised here, and is also quite troubled about the absence of any real discussion of homosexuality within paganism. He urges that this whole area needs much more exploration 'in the context of both opposite and same-sex experiences within the whole spectrum of the spiritual-sexual journey. Continued affirmation of positive erotic expression across the entire sexual spectrum is important.' I agree with this, and would like to see this much better understood.

It seemed that in making these discoveries I had made some sort of breakthrough, but I felt very isolated. I wondered how many other people had thought in this kind of way, and started to look around for support and further guidance. Who in the world was talking about the Goddess and the Horned God? And what was their relation to the feminist insights which were so important for the future of this earth?

# CHAPTER 8

# *Context*

One of the first people I came across was Gary Lingen, who in 1983 had started a magazine called *Newsletter of the Brothers of the Earth*. He, too, had been inspired by Starhawk and others and some of the things he said were mentioned in Chapter 6. For example, he talked about the penis, which we have already seen to be important in understanding the male question, in this way:

> The penis has come in modern times to symbolize power (in very negative ways), domination and conquest over women and children, over other men, and over the Earth. Its positive symbolism and energy must be resurrected as we heal ourselves – our spirits as males – and begin to live in harmony and balance with each other, women, children and the Earth. (Lingen, 1984)

And he got involved with the whole idea of Men's Mysteries, travelling around to Wiccan and other celebrations and organising events for men, usually rather spontaneous and unstructured.

Another writer in the *Newsletter*, which later changed its name to *Brother-song*, made some interesting comments on his own development:

I have heard that at the beginning of the development of the Men's Mysteries, some men had remarked that every time they looked deeply into a god, they'd find a goddess. (Polyandron, 1985)

This had in fact been my experience. I had found it much easier to get in touch with the Goddess than with the God. It had seemed as if I were not ready to get the God yet – the Goddess had to come first.

The author went on to say that he had then discovered a god who could travel between the male and female worlds, and act as a message-bearer:

Hermes can be translated as 'he of the boundary'. He represented a boundary, and at the same time crossed over that boundary, transcending it. That is why he had the power to go from the Earth to Olympus (that is, Heaven), which is represented by his wearing winged sandals, or having wings on his heels. He also was the 'Messenger of the Gods'. Another important attribute was his wand. By its power, also, he could traverse the heavens, the Earth, and enter the Underworld. (Polyandron, 1985)

Now there is a curious connection, which Alan Bleakley points out, between Hermes and the Horned God. The symbol in Astrology for Hermes (known there as Mercury) is ☿ . Bleakley (1984) articulates this, pulling out the presence in this symbol of four aspects of the Horned One: the stag, the ram, the bull and the serpent (Figure 4).

The serpent seems at first the odd one out, but it is found on the *caduceus* (holy wand, still used as a symbol of medicine) and is an important symbol of connection with the Underworld.

On investigating, I found that in Gaul, Cernunnos was associated with Hermes. Analyses of Cernunnos showed the same traits, except that he became the ruler of the Underworld. (Polyandron, 1985)

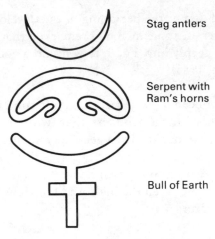

Stag antlers

Serpent with
Ram's horns

Bull of Earth

*Figure 4   Hermes and Cernunnos*

Greeks called Hermes the *Psychopomp* (Conductor of Souls), the same title everywhere given to the Lord of Death in his union with the Lady of Life.

### Whitmont

What I began to learn from this was that there was not just one image of the male which could offer a way out of the masculine dilemma. The world of the Goddess, as Adler (1979) points out again and again, is multiple. The Goddess today takes many forms, each of which has something complementary to offer for women. It should not surprise us, then, that we should come across something multiple in its own way, in the symbolic field of men. Someone who has been arguing for this is Edward Whitmont (1983):

> The new masculine values must respect a variety of different gods or ideals, rather than only one dominant God who is Lord and King.

This sounds promising and insightful, and we look with interest to see what he actually suggests by way of content to fill out this promise. It turns out that he is urging a set of four god-figures (for Jungians all things seem to go in fours) and these are:

Mars, the Roman god of war (and his Greek counterpart Ares), embodies initiating, active energy, courage, determination, desirousness and the impulse toward both work and aggression, including brutality, recklessness and destructive hostility and violence. . . .

Eros is a male phallic deity, an aggressive hunter, he represents the urge to connect, to touch and to possess. He motivates the human quest for humanity, for the beautiful, the good and the divine. . . . He is a son of the Great Mother. . . .

Saturn-Jehovah . . . concretizes, creates and preserves by establishing limits, order and law. He is maker and ruler, the jealous, sick or wounded king or crippled craftsman; ever striving for perfection, he suffers from and tends to deny the flaws of his creations and of existence as it is.

It will be noticed that there are only three figures here, although we were promised four. I wrote to Whitmont about this, and he replied:

I am very grateful to you for catching a textual omission which escaped my editor and myself. I do not know (of course) whether that occurred in the course of retyping or typesetting. Anyway I did not notice it because to me (as to the author always) it was taken for granted. The third masculine type is the original Logos carrier, the Wise Man, Magician, Seer: Tiresias, Merlin, etc., (who corresponds to the feminine Medium type). Thank you for alerting me to that 'hole' in the text. Hopefully it can be straightened out in a later edition. (6 February 1985)

So now we have Mars, Eros, Logos and Saturn-Jehovah. I find this quite a daunting band of heroes, heavy and humourless. Not many dancers here. And this is doubly odd because in other parts of the book Whitmont draws attention to the importance of Dionysus. As we saw earlier, Dionysus is one of the Horned Gods, and a particularly interesting one. Whitmont says:

> The patron of music, drama and intoxication in ancient Greece, the god who dies and is ever reborn, the entity he represents was known under many names among different people: The Horned God, Osiris, Pan, Dumuzi, Azazel, Attis and Tammuz are examples. The most familiar of these to us is the Greek Dionysus.... Of Orpheus, the humanly incarnate form of Dionysus, the legend says that he tamed wild beasts and even the Furies with his music.

And he points out a very interesting fact about the ancient worship of Dionysus, which bears directly on the theme I am trying to tackle in this book. He says:

> The disregard of Dionysus is associated also with a disregard and repression of femininity in its archetypal dimension.
> The Dionysian rites were first and foremost women's rites.

He points out that Dionysus has been depicted as phallus-like, particularly as a giant phallus planted at the doors of Hades, the place of death and renewal.

Hermes, too, is phallic and his *herms* (stone pillars placed at crossroads and other key places all over the classical world) only had two features: a head at the top, and a phallus half way down. As Christianity began to take over, first of all the phalloi were knocked or chiselled off, and in later times crosses were put up to replace the herms, carrying on the tradition.

So if Whitmont agrees that Dionysus and Hermes are important, why are we given Mars, Eros, Logos and Saturn instead? I think we can find an important clue in the work of Nichols (1980), also in the Jungian tradition, where she says:

Psychologically speaking, all the major archetypal figures we have been discussing, being large and powerful, naturally cast shadows commensurate with their size.

The Goddess is usually seen as triune (McLean, 1983; Farrar and Farrar, 1984; Starhawk, 1979) but maybe the God is double. There are some very interesting suggestions along these lines in Miller (1985), and Whitmont (1983) says:

The Goddess is attended by or includes a male counterpart, a phallic or double horned goat, stag or bull god, often split into twin figures of maleness who fight, slay and succeed each other. In later representations, such as the Oedipus myth, they appear as a father-son pair. Eventually they are depicted as twin animals, e.g. two serpents. They complement and serve her in the roles of child, lover, partner, playmate and sacrificial victim. Their cycles of birth, death and rebirth embody the endless tides of physical life.

And here, now, we are right in line with the Craft tradition in Britain, which has always laid a lot of stress on the double nature of the Horned God. For example, Valiente (1984) says this:

Hence the Horned God is the power of returning vitality in the Spring; but he is also the Old God of the Underworld, that Dis from whom, according to Caesar, the Gauls claimed to be descended.

Figure 5 shows one version of this old god. More commonly, the Craft divides the God to represent the two halves of the year, the light half and the dark half. This gives us two god-figures:

The God of the Waxing Year (who appears time and again in mythology as the Oak King) and the God of the Waning Year (the Holly King). They are the light and dark twins, each the other's 'other self', eternal rivals eternally

*Figure 5   Cernunnos as Lord of the Animals from the first-century Gun-destrup Cauldron*

conquering and succeeding each other. (Farrar and Farrar, 1981)

So the twin god is particularly noticed at Midsummer and at Yuletide. The pagan rituals lived on in subtle ways, and we still put out holly at Christmas. In the Yuletide mumming plays, shining St George slays the dark 'Turkish Knight', and then immediately cries out that he has slain his brother. This may remind us of the conflict in the Grail legend of Parzival (von Eschenbach, trans. A.T. Hatto, 1980) between Parzival and Feirefiz. The great Christian knight meets the great Infidel knight on the field of battle – they fight for many hours – then they discover that they are brothers. The poet says:

> Whoever wishes to name them 'two' is entitled to say 'Thus did *they* fight'. Yet they were no more than one ... Each of these unblemished men bore the other's heart within him – theirs was an intimate strangeness!

Now how does all this help to resolve the point we are struggling with – the problem of Mars, Eros, Logos and Saturn? Well, what if each of these were really dual in nature? What if each had a light side and a dark side, as the Jungian thinking would suggest? I played with this idea for a while, and ultimately arrived at some pairs which pleased me: Logos–Dionysus, Eros–Thanatos, Mars–Lucifer, Saturn–Jupiter. But this began to seem like an intellectual exercise without much reality. In particular, it still left out Hermes, who now seems to me quite an important figure.

On a different level, Polyandron (who turned out to be a man named Bruce Baldwin) wrote to me that for him Pan, Hermes, Dionysus and Apollo were the figures who had meant most to him. This seems a much more promising set. Polyandron (1985) says that Freyr is close to Dionysus; Odin is close to Hermes, and so is Loki, and Herne, and Cernunnos. In another way Odin is close to Apollo. It seems that the experiential search is more important than the intellectual search. Polyandron says: 'Somewhere in that "nether region" is the image of myself, of the Horned God, I am seeking. It is not one I can be taught.' (Dionysus and Cernunnos are of course horned gods.)

*Hillman*

Someone who has gone very deeply into these matters is another
Jungian, James Hillman. He has a stunning essay on Dionysus
(Hillman, 1978), where he says that Dionysus has a lot to teach
us about the relations between men and women, showing us
how to get away from misogyny and the male ego. For him, as
for us in this present book, it is all about wounding and healing:

> a psychic affliction would not be divided into a healthy and
> a sick aspect, requiring, thus, a healer and a patient. The
> affliction would not be divided from its own potential of
> nursing, which is constellated by the suffering and the
> childishness. The torn and rendered suffering, rather than
> cured by the medicine of Apollo, becomes an initiation into
> the cosmos of Dionysus.

This theme, of male suffering leading to a new vision, is also
found in another very powerful examination of this area, coming
from Virendra Hills, who lives in Glastonbury. He takes the
work of Perera (1981), which is written for women, and exam-
ines the question of how it can be used by men for their own
development. He says (1983):

> It is only the strong man who will receive the respect and
> attention of the woman who is discovering her own power,
> but what is required of him is that he descend to the depths
> she has been to. Mushy agreements between two half-
> realised people are no longer possible once one of them has
> discovered true strength and identity, and neither can such
> a one be bothered with the immature ego-needs of a partner
> who is afraid to let go of the security of collusive
> compromise.... On the negative side, he must be willing to
> be stripped of all illusions about his masculinity: illusions
> both of his power and dominance, and of his reasonableness
> and righteousness. The woman has always glimpsed the
> truth about the man, but has used considerations of

convenience or fear to avoid admitting it to herself – and certainly to him. Now, when rationality and power and knowledge are combining to threaten the very planet on which these games have been played out for centuries, the time has come for the man to stand naked before the objective eyes of death. There is no other way but down, as the gods of the fathers are revealed as indifferent, afraid or hostile to the shadows cast by their brightness.

Hills emphasises that the vision of the male which emerges from this deep work is not the 'new man' who keeps on being announced in our magazines (e.g. Evans, 1985). Hills says:

The new hero will not be clad in armour, and he will flow around adversaries rather than stand and fight, but he must not be confused with the spuriously gentle man of our time, whose softness protects a core of anger. This man is simply in retreat from the father and from his own aggression and drive, whereas the hero can confront his shadow without flight or resistance or acting-out. Threaten the gentle man and he will either dissolve or hit out blindly. Threaten the hero and he will look inside to see what part of himself is so hidden that it still has power to sneak up on him.

Over and over again we seem to be getting the message that the man who is really going to be able to change his own patriarchal consciousness is the man who is able to go down into the depths.

## Bly

This idea of a dark inner self, a deep inner male, is taken up by Robert Bly in quite another form. Here is someone who has devoted some years to studying the Goddess, and then turned to running workshops where men could discover the inner 'wildman', the deep masculinity which goes beyond merely getting in touch with the inner feminine. For this he goes to a different source again – the fairy tales collected by the Brothers Grimm. These tales were of course handed down by word of mouth, and no one knows just how old they are, or how many generations had heard them before the Grimms wrote them down. The one Bly talks about most is called *Iron John* (or in some versions, *Iron Hans*).

As the story opens, something odd has been happening. Hunters go into the forest near the king's castle, and never come back. Search parties sent after them never come back. Then after many years of leaving the forest alone, a foreign hunter finds the answer. There is something at the bottom of a dark pool that reaches out a long naked arm, and grabs things. The pool is emptied and on the bottom there is lying a wild-looking man, whose body is brown like rusty iron, and whose tangled hair hangs down to his knees. He is bound and led away to the castle, where he is locked up in an iron cage. Bly (1982) says:

> Now let's stop the story here for a second. The implication
> is that when the male looks into his psyche, not being
> instructed what to look for, he may see beyond his feminine
> side, to the other side of the 'deep pool'. What he finds at
> the bottom of his psyche – in this area that no one has visited
> for a long time – is an ancient male covered with hair. Now,
> in all of the mythologies, hair is heavily connected with the
> instinctive, the sexual, the primitive. What I'm proposing is
> that every modern male has, lying at the bottom of his psyche,
> a large, primitive man covered with hair down to his feet.
> Making contact with this wildman is the step the '70s male
> has not yet taken, this is the process that still hasn't taken
> place in contemporary culture.

Bly says that the interior female is challenging and scary enough, but this interior male is even more so for men today. He goes on with the story to show how the king's 8-year-old son opens the cage, frees the wildman, goes off with him and learns valuable lessons from him, also getting help from him at crucial moments in his growing-up process.

My own reaction to this is to feel that something big and important has been touched here. But I am unhappy about the isolation of Iron John. There are no women in this story, except for the princess the young boy eventually marries. We have no hint at all of what this wildman thinks about women. And in fact fairy stories are usually very bad on the question of women. They usually show women as passive, opportunistic or cruel (Kramarae and Treichler, 1985). Two years after the interview just quoted, Bliss (1984) has to say that 'a group in Boston felt the wildman concept gave them permission for sexuality without sensitivity'. And although Bly disapproves of this, and makes a distinction between the Wildman and the Savageman, the opening is there, the confusion is there. What Bly wants is for the Wildman to be the answer to the feminine man, the man who has learned gentleness and nurturance, maybe too well. For these men, who have been down into the pool of femininity, the Wildman is valuable as a corrective, or a further step. But for men who have never done the feminine bit at all, who are unreconstructed male chauvinists, the Wildman is simply an invitation to be even more aggressive. Bly is quoted in Bliss (1984) as saying:

> So one goes from the good boy, which could be the '50s male – very responsible – to the Savageman, which is represented by motorcycle riders or people who hit their wives.

This is a real danger, and it seems much safer to stick to male figures who do have some explicit relationship with the female. With the Horned God this is usually so, and it can certainly be made so for our purposes.

I come back to Hermes again. He can put a light at our feet.

Hermes is our guide between and among all these. He has the power to sympathise with all, to follow all and to enter into all. His mercurial nature enables him to move freely in all directions. As Doty (1980) tells us:

Hermes goes all the way down – into Hades, if you will, certainly into the depths of sleep and psychic movement – before he returns leading the soul-messages (Persephone, Eurydice) back where they can lend insight into the daylight medium and entrapments. That course of movement-downwards can, if we heed the tradition's iconography, be a winged, swift flight across the usual boundaries and limits.

### Stewart

The downward movement is again referred to here, and this leads us on to consider another person who has delved into this area, Bob Stewart. Stewart (1985) has analysed folk songs, which get handed down generation after generation, to find out what they have to say about these matters. What he finds is a consistent story about the UnderWorld and its importance. He calls the Horned God the Great Guardian, and says:

> He is, of course, the Keeper of Animals, the Horned Man. We can find him in a number of forms, partaking mainly of the element of Earth. He is the Keeper of Gateways, the Hunter, a cross between human and horned beast in appearance. His animal parts are bull, deer or goat.

By saying that the Guardian belongs to the UnderWorld, Stewart emphasises that he belongs to the realm of the Goddess, which we noted before was deep and interior. But he says something we have not come across before, and which deserves the closest attention:

> The Horned One is the Arch-Guardian, the Guardian of all guardians who appear within the Tradition. He is not, however, a god who responds to devotion, as does the orthodox image of Christ or of Buddha, or the magical

images of Bel, Lugh, Apollo or Mithras. To worship the Guardian as a god is to misunderstand his function.

He is not solar, says Stewart, nor lunar, nor of the UnderWorld dark gods; he stands between them. He sets up a barrier. The barrier has to be passed, and to do this we have to get past the Guardian:

> In British and European folklore and legend, he must be defeated in a battle of wits, or occasionally a fight of more violent but no more deadly a nature.... The Guardian is that energy or entity between psychic and metaphysical states which turns us back on ourselves. He forbids the passage of any being unable to operate in new dimensions.... In the individual psyche, the ancient Guardian is expressed as that which limits or restricts.... The Guardian stands at the Gateway where we are made fully aware of our own limitations. (Stewart, 1985)

This seems clear enough, and the experience of Stewart himself no doubt bears this out and makes sense of it. But I have to say that this sounds to me much more like Cerberus, or Anubis, or the Celtic Dormarth — a dog or pair of dogs which guard the entrance to the underworld. This dog is to be found on the Gundestrup Cauldron, on which the Horned God is also figured. One of the most familiar images of dogs guarding the gateway is to be found in the Tarot card of the Moon, but none of the commentaries I have seen emphasise that the dogs are there to keep us out. Walker (1983) redresses the balance when she says:

> The dog as keeper of Mother's gate was known everywhere in antiquity, probably because wild dogs were first domesticated as guardians of the home threshold, doorways being generally sacred to the women who owned the houses.

The dog and wolf are of course closely allied, and some versions of the Tarot make one of the dogs into a wolf. The Jim Cleveland pack (Kaplan, 1978) has Anubis guarding the entrance to the land of Kali, the underworld of death and rebirth.

It seems from this that a guardian, and particularly a guardian of the underworld, is much more likely to be a dog than a stag, bull, goat or ram – the particular animals of the Horned God. And in fact a dog would fit much better the character of an entity who can go back and forth between two worlds. A dog is almost proverbially instinctual *and* domesticated, a companion to the living and sensitive to ghosts and strange influences.

In the world of symbols which we are now operating in, animals can be represented by a priestess, shaman or other devotee. The 'false knight upon the road' mentioned in the folk song quoted by Stewart could well be just such a personage. Bleakley (1984), in a suggestive passage, puts forward the idea that the guardian may be a man and a dog together:

At the centre of the World-circle may be found a Fountain of Renewal. It is presided over by a woman, a goddess, and is enclosed within a beautiful garden surrounded by a grove of trees. The fountain is guarded by a black knight and a black dog, consorts to the woman. . . . The knight is a brother, a weird, or other self to each of the journeying knights who seek the fountain; and each will seek combat with this dark brother, unaware that he is a close relative.

This brings us back to the Feirefiz battle which we noticed earlier, and may also remind us of the marvellous Ursula le Guin story *A Wizard of Earthsea*, in which the whole key to the story is a fight to the end between a man and his dark double.

So Stewart leads us into some very stimulating areas. And he makes the very important point that the tradition he is talking about does not have to conflict with Christianity:

The folklorist or anthropologist frequently has to remind self-acclaimed witches that the people who sang folksongs, and who still practise folk rituals were not, generally, practitioners of the old craft as a self-identifying cult. They were, and are, more likely to be practising Christians, with a foundation of the old lore derived from ancestral sources. In the folk memory there is no theoretical conflict between old and new religions; some of Britain's longest-lived pagan ceremonies are faithfully carried out by church or chapel worshippers, and, magically, these ceremonies still work. (Stewart, 1985)

The precise relationship of the pagan ceremonies to Christianity still has to be worked out: certainly in Ireland the Culdee Church combined the two (Adler, 1979). I cannot look at the famous Rublev icon of the Holy Trinity without seeing the triple Goddess. There is the Virgin on the right of the table, in her green gown to represent growth and youth; there is the Mother at the back of the table, in her red gown to represent maturity and childbirth; and there is the Crone on the left of the table, in her more sombre gown to represent old age and wisdom, Sophia. In the centre of the table is the cup, sacred to the female, a prime symbol of the feminine. All three of the figures have magic wands held in their left hands, and the movement round the table is clearly anti-clockwise.

And when Christian mystics talk about God, very often they seem to be talking more about the Goddess:

Such a contemplative person lives in the dynamic, creative presence of God in all things. He may start with a sunset or a small flower. He finds that God is there totally. He no longer feels the need to run frantically throughout the wonders of the world or to exhaust the gamut of human experiences in order to find God. This was perhaps more necessary in the beginning of his prayer life. As persons become more and more advanced in contemplation, especially by the loving presence of the Holy Spirit unifying all things in Christ who leads us to the Heavenly Father, they easily intuit God in all things. Touching anything created yields to them the loving presence of God at the core of all reality. (Maloney, 1979)

It is as if the Holy Trinity, different as it is from the threefold Goddess, somehow by the very fact of its flowingness, its dance, speaks in spite of itself of the Goddess.

This is perhaps only an example of what Wilber (1980) means when he says that all our longings are at bottom just one longing, for ultimate union with the divine and the eternal. All experiential religion, all authentic religion (in terms of Wilber, 1983), is on the same path leading this way. If this is so, pagans do not have to oppose Christianity, just because the Christian church has oppressed and persecuted pagans, and still does.

This is not the place for a full study of comparative religion; we can leave that to theologians like Ruether. But it does seem good at least to acknowledge that something is going on here.

Not only, then, is there a good deal of work being carried on in re-evaluating the position of the male on a spiritual level; but we can also see that none of it is as adequate to the problem in hand as is the approach through the Horned God.

How, then, do we approach the Horned God?

# *Practice*

Initiation is a process of action whereby we pass from one state into another. We come out different on the other side. But because it is a process of action, it takes the form of all other acts. As I have explained in detail elsewhere (Rowan, 1976a), all action takes the form shown in Figure 6. In the present case, we can interpret the boxes like this. The *values* (these are the motivating factors, the drives and desires which move us) have to do with moving along the psychospiritual path of our own development. We want to move beyond the role-bound fixity of having to toe the patriarchal line, or even the 'right-on' anti-patriarchal line laid down by others. We want a direct experience of the deep self behind all the pictures and images.

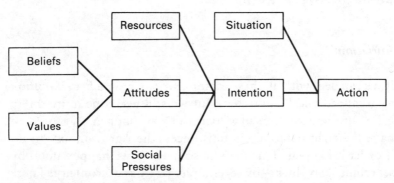

*Figure 6    General theory of action*

The *beliefs* have to do with what leads to what in the world. The argument of this book is that the third way to deal with patriarchal consciousness is to move into the realm of the Goddess and the Horned God. This is safe for women and for the world.

This then yields an *attitude* of being positive about the Goddess and the Horned God, and wanting to get closer to them, know more about them, and ultimately be initiated into their world.

But before this can happen we also need the *resources* to do it. This consists of the requisite time, money, intelligence, knowledge, feeling, intuition – all the things which have to be cultivated before we can pretend to progress. Books like this are one resource; meeting people who are already involved is another resource; doing counselling or therapy gives us more access to our own inner resources; all our past experience, viewed in the right way, can be a resource. We have to build up these resources.

And on the other side, we have to deal with the *social pressures* on us to do or not to do what is needed. The people close to us may not want us to change, or they may be very supportive to us. It is much more difficult to do any action in the world if it is opposed by those who are close to us, whose opinions we value, or who have the power to limit us in various ways. This is an area we have to pay attention to and be realistic about, if we are to move anywhere.

## Initiation

If we can deal with all these factors, we can have a firm *intention* to go ahead and be initiated. But we still need one more thing: a favourable situation in which this can happen. We need to have the right external circumstances, the right context, to do it or let it happen. This may be something we happen upon by searching or by luck – by serendipity or by synchronicity. There is an old occult tradition that when we are ready for the teacher, the teacher appears in our lives. Or we may decide to initiate ourselves. There is an accepted tradition in witchcraft that self-initiation is possible (Buckland, 1974; Valiente, 1978; Farrar and Farrar, 1984). But however we may discover our initiation, it is the readiness which is all. As the diagram makes clear, much has to be prepared before such action is possible.

There are other books which give hints on initiation, and even give some exercises which may be helpful (Matthews and Matthews, 1985; Stewart, 1985) but they are not really oriented towards the demands we have outlined in this book.

One hint which seems noteworthy is the idea that a male is most naturally and ideally initiated by a female. This is a very common belief in Craft circles, and it is easy to see why it should be so. In the present time, however, it seems important not to be dogmatic about this. In every male there is a female, and it may be that she is the person we need to call upon in the present time. And if we as men have to be initiated by a female, why not go direct to the Goddess, and ask her? There are many possibilities here, and to insist on the co-operation of a particular woman seems to be just another instance of patriarchal pressure on women to perform service roles for men.

There is another tradition, explained to me by Peter Dawkins, to which I have no written reference, that initiation should be looked on as a cycle as shown in Figure 7. Our desire for our own development leads to the gaining of the required knowledge, which leads to the ability to serve the Goddess and the Horned God, which leads to the desire to do it better and more fully, which leads to ... and so on. I think this is a valuable notion, because it makes it clear that there is not just one breakthrough, after which we are enlightened or illuminated. There are grades of initiation and stages we have to go through. Wilber (1980) is very clear about this, and Hegel (1974 edn) has this memorable statement:

> This process followed by self-producing Spirit, this path
> taken by it, includes distinct moments; but the path is not
> as yet the goal, the Spirit does not reach the goal without

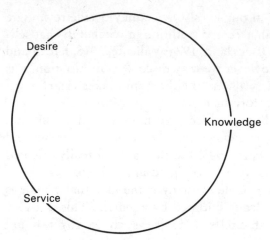

*Figure 7   Model of initiation*

having traversed the path. It is not originally at the goal;
even what is most perfect must traverse the path to the goal
in order to attain it. (Vol.1, p.75)

## A ritual of wounding and healing

As an example of a very simple and basic ritual of initiation,
here is one which emerged from a two-day workshop I organised
in Guildford, consisting entirely of men. This group developed
in a very interesting way, with such differences appearing
between the men that we agreed to do three different rituals –
one for each of the men who wanted to do this – rather than
trying to arrive at one common ritual. Yet when we actually
carried out the three rituals, we found out that all three were
basically the same one ritual, with variations. They were all
about wounding and healing. So what I have tried to do here is
to consolidate the most effective features of the three rituals into
one.

Wallace (1966) says that the most powerful rituals have five stages, and I have tried to follow his plan in what follows. The five stages are:

1 *Pre-learning* A person is taught about the problem to be dealt with, and all the details are brought to mind. The person is also told the solution to the problem, but at this stage it does not help in any way. This is a stage just of soaking in the problem itself.
2 *Separation* The person is subjected to isolation, darkness, loud noise, monotonous or repetitive stimuli, disorienting drugs or to stress. The person does not see the point of these exercises, and is confused and upset. This is a loosening or unfreezing or chaotic stage. It is all about letting go.
3 *Suggestion* The person is presented with the assurance that the transformation has been accomplished, and the prelearned solution has now been so appropriated as to become a part of the personality or character of the person.
4 *Execution* The person is then given an opportunity to act in the new way implied by his transformation.
5 *Maintenance* The person is reminded of their changed state and encouraged to find ways of expressing it in everyday life. This reinforces the effect of the ritual and deepens it.

Horne (1978) points out that these five stages parallel in an interesting way the five stages of growth of the mystic, as explained by Underhill (1961). She calls them, in order, Awakening, Purgation, Illumination, Dark Night of the Soul, and the Unitive Life. There are also, of course, interesting parallels here with the process of psychotherapy – though the differences are important, too.

With so much as preliminary, here is the actual ritual. It is offered as a suggestion specifically for men who want to work on the very thorny issues of feminism. Whether it is useful for anyone else, or for any other topic, I do not know. For its chosen purpose, it seems to be very effective.

### Phase 1    The wounding

The man (this is what the focal person will be called throughout) puts together all the accusations he can think of – from memory, from letters, from books, articles, news items or wherever. These are the things which the man feels guilty about, or gets continually criticised for. If the former, the accusations may be in the form of questions: *How have you hurt women? How have you hurt children? How have you hurt other men? How have you been untrue to the best in you?* If the latter, the accusations may be in the form of judgments: *You don't listen to women. You don't let women in. You put women down. You should be more responsible. You exploit women. You should give up pornography. Stop raping your wife.* (I have put here a number of feminist accusations, but in practice the men wanted to include other things too, such as: *Put up a shelf. Have the answers. Get everyone there on time. Don't make mistakes.* These are all self-oppressive statements. This is OK and should be allowed for the maximum effect – the man has to feel that the accusations are personal to him.)

These are then distributed to the other members of the group, and the man becomes the centre of attention, and arranges the set-up. The accusers may walk round the man in a circle, or may sit facing him on the floor, or on chairs, or behind tables, or on a dais – whatever is most menacing, threatening or otherwise evocative for the man concerned. They may be dressed as men or as women. The man may stand or kneel, or take up whatever posture seems most vulnerable or defenceless.

This phase should somehow rise to a climax, and loud music may be useful in this. But the climax can be quite different. In one case we had a court of law set-up, and the climax was when one of the assessors said – 'I now sentence you to the maximum penalty within our power: you shall live in the body of A.... B.... and take on all his history for as long as you shall live.' Imagination can dictate what the climax should be in each case.

*Phase 2   The silence*

Phase 1 builds to a climax, and then there is a silence. In the silence the group may leave the room or the room may be darkened, or the man may be bound, yoked, blindfolded or hooded – again whatever seems most effective for the man concerned.

The man lets the accusations sink in, and goes to the bottom with them in open self-examination and vulnerable self-criticism. This is a key point in the whole ritual, and it must not be shortened.

At a certain point a turn upwards will be experienced – a lightening of the spirit. When this reaches the point where the man is able to accept human contact, he gives a prearranged signal. This may be just intense breathing, or it may be a word or phrase, or a song or chant – anything at all which may seem suitable.

On the signal the others return and come close to the person. Words and gentle physical contact follow. Light touches or strokes are better than hugs, holds or grips at this stage. The words are words of forgiveness: *You don't have to be perfect. You are a good man. You don't have to control everything. I understand why you did what you did. Everybody makes mistakes. You did the best you could – could any of us say more? No blame. You don't have to get it right all the time.* But each person must take responsibility only to say what they really believe and can say from the heart. No phony reassurance is required or useful.

*Phase 3   The healing*

Now the lights are restored, the blindfold taken off, the bonds removed, the yoke taken off – maybe the person changes clothes. Again this is up to the man to specify and determine. Clothes can be very symbolic, but they do not mean the same thing to everybody.

And the man is welcomed to the group, in whatever way seems appropriate. It is good to be spontaneous here, and make use of whatever is going on or whatever is available to express welcome and joy. For one man a solemn procession may be best, for another a dance, for another a chorus or chant. Whatever is done should enable the man to feel a sense of dropping the past and living in the present. For example, at this point for one man a thunder-storm started, and he was led out into it by the group for ritual cleansing and refreshment on a hot day.

A sense of acceptance by the group is the key thing here. Music may again be useful – this time cheerful lilting music, good-humoured and flowing.

### Phase 4    Application
Now the group disperses into the four corners of the room or into four groups not too far apart. The man goes to the first group and says: 'Here is the situation. Here is what I do now.' He describes one of the situations in which the previous accusations applied. But this time he describes a new way of handling the situation, which means that the accusation will not arise.

If this is convincing, the group says – 'So may it be' – and the man goes on to the next group. If it seems questionable in any way, the group questions it until a satisfactory solution is reached. It is very important that these applications are as realistic as possible. If the group cannot be satisfied the man goes on to the next group with a new situation, and later comes back to the rejecting group with another situation or with a better version of the original one.

When all are satisfied, the man goes into the centre and waits.

### Phase 5    Maintenance
The whole group now gathers round and asks the man questions like this: *How will you keep this up when you get back home? How could you ruin it all again? What would help you to remember what you have learned? Name three ways of sabotaging your solutions. How can you get others to help you in retaining this change? What resources do you need to keep this up, and how are you going to get them?*

When all are convinced that the man really has worked out good ways of maintaining the gains made in the ritual, the ritual ends. There may be a group hug or some other suitable ending acceptable to the man.

If people in the group have feelings stirred up by this ceremony, they may work on these feelings in pairs to arrive at some conclusion. There should then be a complete break before anything else is done.

### Some general points

When we did it, each ceremony took about an hour, but it seems more realistic to allow more time, so that there is a sense of being able to do each part thoroughly and have some time afterwards for relaxation and digestion.

It is important to realise that this is not psychotherapy. It is working in archetypal forms: first the archetype of the accuser – here particularly the accusing female, the virago, the angry woman; then the archetype of despair (here there is a similarity to the workshops of Macy (1983)); and then the archetype of initiation and acceptance, of entry into the bosom of the group, or of the tribe. The archetype of wounding and healing, most of all.

The reason for publishing this is so that other groups – particularly men's groups – can pick it up and adapt it to their own needs. Work in this area is much needed, if we are successfully to question patriarchy and its existing establishment.

### Despair and empowerment

The work of Joanna Macy, just mentioned, is of great interest. What she has done is to take the big issues of today – ecology, waste of the earth's resources, poverty, overpopulation and most of all nuclear war – and to run workshops where people are encouraged to get in touch with their real feelings about these matters. Almost invariably, the main feeling turns out to be despair. Not an individual despair - 'Oh, you're depressed at the moment' – but a deep pain for the world. In her workshops people are encouraged to go into this despair, really experiencing it and owning up to it, and then coming out of it on the other side. And when this is done, it seems that people almost always come out stronger, feeling that they can link with other people in a network of mutual support and empowerment, to do something about it.

This work has resulted in a worldwide network called *interhelp*, which consists of people who have been through such an initiation, such a ritual – because in the bigger workshops, which go on longer, there is a definite ritual element which can come in. One of the exercises which is done is the Despair Ritual developed by Chellis Glendinning after the Three Mile Island nuclear power station accident.

In this ritual there are three concentric circles of people. In the beginning, everyone gets into the outer ring, which is the Circle of Reporting. They spontaneously come out with whatever is on their minds about the condition of the world. As each person does this, the others listen, and reply, 'Indeed, it is so.'

When feelings are aroused by this, people who feel so moved can go into the middle ring, the Circle of Anger and Fear. Here they stamp, hit cushions, tremble and walk, scream out their feelings – just release their terrible tensions in whatever way seems right for them.

In the centre is the Circle of Sorrow, piled with cushions or pillows, where a quieter grief may be expressed. Here people may be sobbing or holding each other or huddling on their own. People move into this circle as and when they feel moved to do so.

At a certain point, unprogrammed and unled, the mood gradually changes. The Circle of Reporting starts to utter some more positive messages, of compassion, of fellow-feeling, of hope. This comes out of the experience of commonality, of discovering that one is not alone. As the positive messages are heard and responded to – 'Indeed, it is so' – relief may start to break out. Songs may start – there are many different things which can happen, because the leader (or roadperson, as Glendinning says) does not programme anything except the three circles and the basic discipline of 'Indeed, it is so'.

It is easy to see the parallels with our work here. Patriarchal consciousness, in all its forms, is as big a threat as nuclear war – in fact, it is the basic cause of nuclear war, in its linear defensive thinking, and in its seduction by technology as the answer to everything.

If we can face up to patriarchal consciousness – and this is more difficult than facing up to nuclear war, because it is inside us as well as outside us – we can use the basic principles of Macy's work to create our own rituals and ceremonies.

## Wrestling with the Horned God

When it comes to the Horned God, we cannot simply rely on the established forms of Wicca. The Craft was not designed to overthrow patriarchy, it was designed to ignore patriarchy. If we want to use the Horned God as our gateway, we have to be much more conscious than Craft people usually are of the possibilities of patriarchal subversion within witchcraft.

As I have gone around talking to witches, many of the women have told me of men who used the Craft as just another way of getting and using patriarchal power. The possibilities of self-deception are enormous. I met one man who talked with stars in his eyes of how his spiritual strength for combating sexism had gained from his work in a coven. Then I heard from a woman that he had had sex with every woman in that coven, including two lesbians, and had made two of them pregnant, including one of the lesbians. Most importantly, none of them were speaking to him any longer.

Another man I heard of had started as a powerful anti-sexist man, and had then got into sex magic, in a way which made some women quite suspicious.

I don't think there is any easy solution to this problem. We as men are so heavily imbued with patriarchal consciousness that we are likely to fall, again and again, into patriarchal ways which exploit women all over again by new means. It seems to be a fact that every effort which men make to deal with their patriarchal consciousness has the effect of making them more attractive to women. When a man does not hate and fear women, it shows, and many women like it. But obviously this increases the potential for sexual exploitation, because under patriarchy heterosexual sex is a much better deal for men than it is for women.

I can't think of a single rule which would make this situation a safe one. Some feminists have suggested that the answer is to be celibate, but I don't believe this can be a real answer for more than a tiny minority of people. While patriarchy rules, men are just in a privileged position, and that's it. It seems deeply unfair, but it is up to us as men not to exploit that unfairness. To the extent that we are plugged in to the deep female energy of the Goddess, it will be easier. To the extent that we have got in touch with our own female energy, it will be easier. To the extent that we have a conscious awareness of our own actions, it will be easier.

My own practice is to have just one intimate relationship with a woman. She goes out to work and has a senior position in her job. I stay at home and do the Hoovering and the dusting and polishing and wiping and washing up, and see my clients and write, and go out to give lectures and run groups. We pay equally for most things, except that where I use something more (like the telephone) I pay more for it. We set aside time to see each other so that it does not just happen by chance. It is the most equal relationship I have ever had. It is made easier by the fact that I have had a vasectomy and she doesn't want to have children. This makes us quite a special case, I realise, and not typical or capable of standing as an example to all. In a sense she is the Goddess and I am the Horned God. In another sense we are people fumbling around trying to make sense of an impossible situation. As one of Beckett's characters once said – 'I can't go on. I'll go on.'

# CHAPTER 10

# A *way* forward

When women realise what patriarchal consciousness is and does, they feel a terrible, terrible pain which extends into every corner of their lives. They realise how many putdowns, how many slights, how many harassments, how many threats, how many blows, how many mutilations, how many rapes, how many deaths are suffered by women, If anyone doubts this, let them go to the classics of feminism – Brownmiller (1976), Chicago (1979), Daly (1979), Dworkin (1974), Lederer (1980), Rhodes and McNeill (1985) and the rest.

When men realise what patriarchal consciousness is and does, their feelings are much more varied and complicated. My own first reaction was to say, 'How awful for them. Something must be done about this.' Then I went through, 'The liberation of oppressed people must be the work of those people themselves. All I can do is to support their struggle as and when invited to do so.' Then I went through, 'Men are twisted and limited in very important and crippling ways under patriarchy. Let's do something about that.' Then I went through, 'It's all no good. There is nothing that can be done. The system is too big. Its supporters are everywhere. Maybe I am one too. There is no hope.' Then I went through, 'Now that I don't hate women, things look more hopeful. But now that I can feel their pain, I realise that things are much worse than I could conceive of before. And now I realise that my own pain about my father is worse than I thought, too.' And then I came to, 'It is not just about individual fathers and mothers, or even about social problems on a large scale which are oppressive – it's about deep archetypes where the pain is on a cosmic scale. The depths we have to go into are much deeper than we thought, and the dangers are not just physical dangers or mental dangers, but spiritual dangers too.' And it was not until I got to that last point that I began to feel that I had got anywhere at all.

It is this experience which leads me to believe that meeting and dealing with patriarchal consciousness is more difficult for men than it is for women. We as men seem to have to go through a much more tortuous process than the relatively direct route open to women. And because less has been written about the archetypal level of response than about the other two levels (conscious-political and unconscious-therapeutic), I want to focus more particularly on that.

### Male and female

We saw earlier, in a chapter which may have seemed rather negative, that the idea of androgyny, while very valuable at a therapeutic level (healing the splits in the personality and all that), will not do at the spiritual-political level which we have now reached. So if androgyny won't do, what will do?

The account which fitted best with my own experience, and seemed to illuminate it further, I found in Alan Bleakley's (1984) book, *Fruits of the Moon Tree*. This is a Christmas pudding of a book, indigestible in large quantities, delicious in small spoonfuls, and with the odd threepenny bit here and there.

Bleakley says that if we take a bit of elastic (or a guitar string, etc.) and hold it stretched loosely between our two hands, and pluck it (or get someone else to pluck it) nothing much will happen. But if we stretch it tight and do the same thing, we will get a musical note. If we stretch it further, too far, it will snap, and again no music.

If the two hands represent the male and female poles of

experience (Bleakley says masculine and feminine, following I suppose Jung, but I have argued against that terminology) then we have an interesting analogy. If the male and female poles are too close together, this could be a crude attempt at fusion, or perhaps androgyny – the liberal pretence that there is really no difference, that we should talk about people's liberation rather than women's liberation, and so on. No music – no creative outcome – can result from this.

Similarly, if the male and the female poles get too far apart, and the string snaps, this could be the situation where men retire into their clubs, and women into their sororities – the men cultivate war while the women cultivate peace – the two do not meet, and again no music results. (On a temporary basis it may make a lot of sense for women to separate, in order to work out things which they cannot work out in the presence of men, but we are talking here about more long-term truths.)

But if we pull the male and female poles far enough apart for each of them to differentiate and work out their full essence, without losing touch with each other, then some creative outcome can result.

Bleakley carefully points out that this is true within each person as well as between people and between groups of people. The contrasexual archetypes within each person also work in this way. Thus each man needs to cultivate, get to know, allow to develop and encourage the female inside himself. This is not necessarily easy to do. I remember one time when I tried to do this, the female who came out was the one who hated and feared men. I found that this was my twin sister, who I had killed in the womb in order to ensure my own survival. In the therapy group, I then had to enact a ritual where I went back into the womb, and this time rescued my sister, and made sure that she was born with me. This produced such extreme feelings of relief, and such a further improvement in my relations with women, that I feel there must have been something in it.

What comes out of Bleakley's analysis is a very strong emphasis on the importance of difference. We have to differentiate before we can integrate. Kate Millett (1971) says:

> Because of our social circumstances, male and female are
> really two different cultures, and their life experiences are
> utterly different – and this is crucial.

We have to recognise this, much better than we usually do at
the moment. But to recognise it is not to lose hope about it. It
is to see that difference as the very heart of the answer. The
wounds of feminism can only be healed by deeper feminism.
Difference, as Audre Lorde (1981) tells us, is:

> a fund of necessary polarities between which our creativity
> can spark like a dialectic. . . . Only within that
> interdependency of different strengths, acknowledged and
> equal, can the power to seek new ways to actively 'be' in
> the world generate, as well as the courage and sustenance to
> act where there are no charters. . . . Difference is that raw
> and powerful connection from which our personal power is
> forged.

So what does this actually mean in terms of the relation of
female to male and male to female? It means that we as men
have to become much more aware of how different we are, and
how heavy that can seem to women, and how problematical it
is to be a man. No longer can we take it for granted that we
know what it is to be a man. We have to open our eyes to our
own nature and conditioning. We have to wake up from our
semi-hypnotic state.

Our difference from women means that we have to be very
careful how we talk about feminism and approach feminists.
Bruce Woodcock (1984) made a very important point about this:

> Claims as to the values and goals of feminism have a quite
> different function and meaning when women make them on
> their own behalf than they do when men make them. When
> women assert values as 'feminist' or 'female', even those
> which have been traditionally ascribed to them within
> patriarchal ideology, their activity declares a conception of

themselves as part of a process of self-definition. When a man adopts the same arguments, their political function changes quite simply because of the relationship between those arguments, whose aim is to challenge male power, and male power itself. One must inevitably suspect a conscious or unconscious attempt to contain their impact, or somehow subvert or appropriate the cutting edge of feminism by containing it within male-defined limits.

That is why, in this book, I have tried to talk not about feminism, or about women's experience, but about men's experience, and about male responses to what men understand by feminism in its critique of patriarchal consciousness.

I am saying that in my own response to that critique, I have been most inspired by the power of the spiritual insights of people like Starhawk and the authors in Spretnak (1982) and by Hills (1983). My spirit rises when I hear Starhawk saying that the Horned God can make men

> free to be wild without being cruel, angry without being violent, sexual without being coercive, spiritual without being unsexed, and able to truly love.

Figure 8 (p. 142) shows a modern vision of the Horned God. The emphasis on polarity, on difference, makes it very natural to see sex as polarity, sex as difference, and to know that

> In its essence, it is not limited to the physical act – it is an exchange of energy, of subtle nourishment, between people. Through connection with another, we connect with all. (Starhawk, 1979)

And this way of putting it means that we do not have to see it as just heterosexual – such a statement can be just as true for bisexual, gay or lesbian sex.

In a way, though I am quite nervous about putting it this way, we are talking about a third sexual revolution. The first was about getting rid of Victorian fear and hypocrisy – just bringing things out in the open, and freeing people from harmful guilt. That revolution was going on all through the 1920s, and right up to its culmination in the 1960s with the discovery of the Pill. It is still continuing today, though now there is a backlash as well.

The second sexual revolution was about women starting to notice that the whole thing had been organised by men, with male assumptions and male values, for the benefit of men. The way in which women had been supposed to participate was by being just like men in every way. And indeed the notion of unisex which was prevalent in the 1960s was very much on these lines – both sexes were to dress like men, think like men and behave like men (men in pink shirts and flowered ties, to be sure). But women, now able to explore their own sexuality more freely, found that it was not a mere replica of male sexuality – it was both different and more varied. And this was discovered not in a spirit of pure objectivity, but in a context of resentment. Resentment at men for the way in which they had offered sexual freedom on their own terms, in ways which favoured them, and which gave them the advantage in terms of power and control. What women demanded was to be seen as persons with their own female culture, just as real and just as deep as the dominant male culture, but far less well known and far harder to be clear about. Their message to men was – 'Lay off until I am clearer about what I myself want. Maybe I want sex with a man, maybe I want sex with another woman, maybe I want sex by myself; maybe I don't want sex at all. Maybe it's important to me, and maybe it isn't. Let me find out.' For many men, this was confusing and frustrating. They had just woken up to the glories of the first sexual revolution, and now here was the second, which seemed to take them all away again. We are still working through all the implications of this second revolution. Because men own and control the media, many men still haven't heard of this revolution, but they will, they will.

Now since this second revolution is still not finished – indeed, in many ways it has hardly begun – it may seem premature to talk about a third. This is especially so for men, since there are very few writings about the second sexual revolution for men – perhaps only Reynaud (1983) and a few others get near it. The third revolution has been even less talked about, and is little known. But if Starhawk (1982) is right, and if 'potentially, the erotic bond could be the model for all other associations, all connections in freedom', then it seems worthwhile to at least look a bit further in that direction. When someone says:

> Alice and I went to bed and made love, and it was very different for me from what it usually is. I wasn't tense at all and I just let myself go. Alice and I seemed to merge into one, our breathing became synchronized and then we seemed to become attuned to the rhythms of nature that surrounded us, the distant Atlantic breakers, the wind blowing across the island, the pulsing of the stars. When I came, it wasn't just a tension release, but like the exploding of the universe inside me. (Ken, in James, 1985)

What are we to make of this? Is it just a good orgasm, where the earth moves? Is it just a Reichian orgasm, where the whole body surrenders? Or is it cosmic sex, where a creative and spiritual experience emerges from the polarities in tension? I see it as pointing to the possibility of a third sexual revolution, where by invoking the earth powers of the Goddess and the Horned God, we allow sex to become the archetypal union of opposites that it fundamentally is.

In this way we would see the aim as being not androgyny but the *hieros gamos*, the *conjunctio* in alchemy, the sacred marriage.

### Hieros gamos

This is the Greek name for the union of a king or sacred king (surrogate for the real king) with his Goddess, usually in the form of a priestess-queen impersonating the Goddess. The sacred marriage was once considered essential to the king's right to rule. As Barbara Walker (1983) tells us:

> British romances show kings unable to rule unless they possessed the queen, whose name was often given as Guinevere – also rendered Cunneware, Gwenhwyfar, Jennifer, Ginevra or Genevieve. Some early sources say that there were three of her (the Triple Goddess). King Arthur married all three. Repeated abductions of her by Meleagant, by Lancelot, by Melwas, by Arthur and by Mordred signified many would-be kings' claim to sovereignty. The collapse of Arthur's kingdom was intimately related to the loss of the queen.

This makes it clear that the sacred marriage was a form of initiation. Henderson (1964) tells us that

> the novice for initiation is called upon to give up willful ambition and all desire and to submit to the ordeal. He must be willing to experience this trial without hope of success. In fact, he must be prepared to die; and though the token of his ordeal may be mild (a period of fasting, the knocking out of a tooth, or tattooing) or agonizing (the inflictions of the wounds of circumcision, subincision or other mutilations), the purpose remains always the same: to create the symbolic mood of death from which may spring the symbolic mood of rebirth.

Again we find that these perhaps rather mysterious words are illuminated by actually current pagan practice. In the Wicca tradition, a High Priestess and a High Priest are normally present, but in the absence of one of them a difference appears. A valid ceremony can be held with only a High Priestess, but if only a High Priest is present, no valid ceremony can be held. As the Farrars (1984) put it:

They are essential to each other, and ultimately equal (remembering that the immortal Individuality, the reincarnating monad, is hermaphroditic), but in the context of Wiccan working and of their present incarnation, he is rather like the Prince Consort of a reigning Queen. He is (or should be) a channel for the God aspect, and there is nothing inferior about that; but Wiccan working is primarily concerned with the 'gifts of the Goddess', so the Priestess takes precedence; for woman is the gateway to witchcraft, and man is her 'guardian and student'.

This relationship, which involves a man giving up his 'healthy male ego' and surrendering to the Goddess – and going through a rebirth as a result – is what makes pagan religion safe for the earth. A man in that relationship cannot risk destroying the earth, for the Earth is the Goddess. A man in that relationship cannot seek to outdo the creativity, or the destruction, of the Goddess, as the atomic scientists described in Easlee (1983) tried to do.

And this can go further. By focussing on the *hieros gamos*, we can rescue the father. One of the tragedies of the anti-sexist men's movement is that it has so often downplayed and looked askance at the father. Even the word 'patriarchal', which we defended earlier, seems to be saying that fathers are bad. But Perry (1966) reminds us that:

Among the principal functions of the Royal Father in the archaic era was his performance of the rite of the sacred marriage with the queen (or perhaps the priestess) which represented the Father God and the Mother Goddess in their *hieros gamos*. At the level of earth cult this was obviously designed to promote the invigoration of the life force and fertility in which sexual union means the propagation of life. However, the union of male and female came to signify much more than procreation during the archaic era. It gathered many meanings of a mythological and cosmological dimension, such as the union, balance and harmony of opposites thus comprising the image of wholeness and completion. The Chinese *Chou-li* said of the position of the overlord, 'There Heaven and Earth are united: there the four seasons are at one: ... there, the Yin and the Yang are in harmony'; the Indian *Satapatha Brahmana* said of the role of the queen, 'For she, inasmuch as she is his wife, is half of himself ... in finding a wife he is born, for then he becomes complete.'

This means that we can not only be sons and lovers of the Goddess, but also fathers in relation to the Mother. The father is OK. One of the great documents of ancient times speaks of the marriage of Inanna (Kramer, 1969; Wolkstein and Kramer, 1985), and her husband Dumuzi is one of the names by which the Horned God is invoked in pagan ceremonies.

But the god is never self-sufficient. At the moment that he tries to be self-sufficient, the Goddess will drag him down, as Perera (1981) makes clear. He must be connected to the Goddess. In talking of the Sky God, James (1963) tells us that he must be connected to his Shakti if he is going to be active. As Walker (1983) explains, Shakti is the tantric version of the Great Goddess, realised both as a sexual partner and as the innermost, animating soul of man or god. 'Every god needed his Shakti, or he was powerless to act.' An ancient tantric text says that not even God could become the supreme Lord unless Shakti entered into him. 'As the god required her power before he could do anything at all, so her worshipper on earth required the power of his own Istadevata, Shakti or lady-love.'

The male counterpart of Shakti is Shiva, and Bleakley (1984) prints side by side the two pictures of Shiva from the Mohenjo-Daro excavations, and of Cernunnos from the Gundestrup cauldron. He says:

The Hindu Shiva, as Pasupati (lord of animals), and Cernunnon, a Celtic variant of Mercury, are shown in similar postures, wearing an animal-horn headdress and stag's antlers respectively, and surrounded by animals.

So Shiva, a horned god, relates to Shakti as divine universal force or energy. Durdin-Robertson (1976) tells us that a much esteemed medieval ode to the Goddess in India says, 'If Shiva is united with Shakti, he is able to exert his power as lord; if not, the god is not able to stir.'

If we as men deliberately and consciously take up this position, going through the initiations, the death-and-rebirth conditions required to do so, then we shall be fit to live in a post-patriarchal world. We have to go beyond patriarchy and matriarchy to what lies beyond, but at this point in history it is the female principle which needs to be put first.

## A way forward

So it is time now to draw the threads together, and examine the design we have now discovered. What must a man do, in realistic terms?

First, he must admit that there is such a thing as patriarchal consciousness, and that he is a living example of how oppressive it can be. He has to learn from women what that oppression feels like, and how he contributes to it. He has to agree to be wounded by this knowledge, and to feel the pain of that realisation.

Second, he must do what he can at a conscious and political level to change the patriarchal world – to make new laws, new rules, new organisational forms, or whatever is needed to make the life-chances of women more equal and more fair, and to stop them being exploited, threatened and attacked. He can give emotional support to women, to the extent that they permit that.

Third, he must work on himself at an unconscious level, to remove his resistances to taking the second step. The reason why the second step is so limited in the world is because the third step has not been taken. (In most cases the first step has not been taken either.) He will discover how to relate better to himself, to women, to men and to children. He will find out more about his internal female, and how to relate to her. He will discover the whole great world of feelings – his own and other people's.

Fourth, he must work on himself at a spiritual level, first of all getting in touch with his own real self, and then daring to die all over again by going into the world of the Goddess, and being reborn as the Horned God, who can relate to the Goddess in a complementary and helpful way, while regaining that full maleness he had questioned and perhaps lost along the way. He can find that deep masculinity that lies on the other side of the female. He can draw on female energy without exploiting females.

Fifth, he is then fit to relate to feminists and enter into dialogue with them. It may be that feminists can make a new world without male allies, but I don't see it as very likely. And if there are to be such allies, they can only be men who have been through that whole process of development. Only such men can enter into genuine dialogue with women who want to dismantle patriarchy. By recognising that such women are invoking the power of the Goddess, men can relate to them as guardians and as students.

By doing this, men can gain immeasurably, because instead of seeing power as essentially male and essentially untrustworthy, they can relate instead to the much deeper and stronger female power – the power of the Shakti. What I have tried to do in this book is to show how men can co-operate in this process without losing their male quality, and gaining something quite new. The Horned God, as Starhawk (1979) reminds us, is untamed:

> He is all that within us that will never be domesticated, that refuses to be compromised, diluted, made safe, moulded or tampered with. He is free.

But we cannot end there, because we are still faced with patriarchy. We cannot really be free while this system remains. So we are left with the pain of awareness. Now, however, we

can live better with this pain because we have faced and dealt
with our own responses to it. Whatever we do now must be
illuminated by a fresh light because of that. And we can now
reach out for the support of others in a worldwide network of
hope, soundly based in despair. For us now, hope can never be
an illusory thing; it is something we create by our intentions
and by our projects. It can include the living strength we get
from the Great Goddess, and it can include the inspiration of
the Horned God. Together we can be consciously aware of the
social processes which are about to bring patriarchy to an end,
and we can take a more active part in hastening that end.

# KERNUNNOS

Figure 8    *Contemporary portrait of Cernunnos by Morning Glory Zell, 1983*

# Bibliography

Adcock, Cynthia (1982), 'Fear of "Other": The common root of sexism and militarism', in Pam McAllister (ed.), *Reweaving the Web of Life: Feminism and Nonviolence*, Philadelphia: New Society Publishers.

Adler, Margot (1979), *Drawing Down the Moon: Witches, Druids, Goddess-worshippers and Other Pagans in America Today*, Boston: Beacon Press.

Alderfer, Clayton P. (1972), *Existence, Relatedness, Growth*, New York: Collier-Macmillan.

Bach, George and Wyden, Peter (1969), *The Intimate Enemy: How to Fight Fair in Love and Marriage*, New York: William Morrow.

Baynes, C. F. (1968), *I Ching or Book of Changes*, London: Routledge & Kegan Paul.

Bem, Sandra (1974), 'The measurement of psychological androgyny', *Journal of Consulting and Clinical Psychology*, 44, 155–62.

Bem, Sandra (1977), 'Beyond androgyny: Some presumptuous prescriptions for a liberated sexual identity' in C. G. Carney and S. L. McMahon (eds), *Exploring Contemporary Male/Female Roles: A Facilitator's Guide*, La Jolla: University Associates

Bianchi, Eugene (1976), 'Psychic celibacy and the quest for mutuality' in E. C. Bianchi and R. R. Ruether, *From Machismo to Mutuality*, New York: Paulist Press.

Bleakley, Alan (1984), *Fruits of the Moon Tree*, London: Gateway Books.

Bliss, Shepherd (1984), 'Robert Bly: Controversial poet of love and grief', *Yoga Journal*, Sept/Oct.

Bly, Robert (1982), 'What men really want', Interviewed by Keith Thompson in *New Age*, May, 30–51.

Brothers, Joyce (1982), *What Every Woman Should Know About Men*, London: Granada.

Broverman, I. K. *et al.* (1970), 'Sex role stereotypes and clinical judgements of mental health', *Journal of Consulting and Clinical Psychology*, 34, 1–7

Brownmiller, Susan (1976), *Against our Will: Men, Women and Rape*, Harmondsworth: Penguin.

Buckland, Raymond (1974), *The Tree: The Complete Book of Saxon Witchcraft*, New York: Samuel Weiser.

Chicago, Judy (1979), *The Dinner Party*, Garden City: Anchor Books.

Chicago, Judy (1980), *Embroidering our Heritage: The Dinner Party Needlework*, Garden City: Anchor Books.

Christ, Carol P. (1980), *Diving Deep and Surfacing: Women Writers on Spiritual Quest*, Boston: Beacon Press.

Colegrave, Sukie (1979), *The Spirit of the Valley: Androgyny and Chinese Thought*, London: Virago.

Daly, Mary (1973), *Beyond God the Father: Towards a Philosophy of Women's Liberation*, Boston: Beacon Press.

Daly, Mary (1979), *Gyn/Ecology*, Boston: Beacon Press.

Daly, Mary (1984), *Pure Lust*, London: The Women's Press.

Demause, Lloyd (1984), *Reagan's America*, New York: Creative Roots.

Doty, W. G. (1980), 'Hermes' heteronymous appellations', in J. Hillman (ed.), *Facing the Gods*, Irving: Spring Publications.

Dryden, W. (ed.) (in press), *Key Cases in Psychotherapy*, London: Harper & Row.

Duberman, Lucille (1975), *Gender and Sex in Society*, New York: Praeger.

Dunayevskaya, Raya (1981), *Rosa Luxemburg, Women's Liberation and Marx's Philosophy of Revolution*, Brighton: Harvester Press.

Durdin-Robertson, Lawrence (1976), *The Goddesses of India, Tibet, China and Japan*, Clonegal: Cesara Publications.

Dworkin, Andrea (1974), *Woman Hating*, New York: E. P. Dutton.

Easlee, Brian (1983), *Fathering the Unthinkable: Masculinity, Scientists and the Nuclear Arms Race*, London: Pluto Press.

Ernst, Sheila and Goodison, Lucy (1981), *In Our Own Hands: A Book of Self-help Therapy*, London: The Women's Press.

Evans, Peter (1985), 'Make way for the new man', *Listener*, 4 July, 4/2916.

Evison, Rose and Horobin, Richard (1983), *How to Change Yourself and Your World*, Sheffield: Co-counselling Phoenix.

Farrar, J. and S. (1981), *Eight Sabbats for Witches*, London: Robert Hale.

Farrar, J. and S. (1984), *The Witches' Way: Principles, Rituals and Beliefs of Modern Witchcraft*, London: Robert Hale.

Farrell, Warren (1975), *The Liberated Man*, New York: Bantam.

Fasteau, Marc Feigen (1975), *The Male Machine*, New York: Dell.

Fordyce, J. K. and Weil, R. (1971), *Managing with People*, Reading: Addison-Wesley.

Fromm, Erich (1942), *The Fear of Freedom*, London: Routledge & Kegan Paul.

Gardner, Gerald B. (1954), *Witchcraft Today*, New York: Magickal Childe.

Gardner, Gerald B. (1959), *The Meaning of Witchcraft*, New York: Magickal Childe.

Goldberg, H. (1980), *The New Male*, New York: Signet.

Goldenberg, Naomi R. (1979), *Changing of the Gods: Feminism and the End of Traditional Religions*, Boston: Beacon Press.

Goodman, A. and Walby, P. (1975), *A Book About Men*, London: Quartet.

Göttner-Abendroth, Heide (1985), 'Thou Gaia art I. Matriarchal mythology in former times and today', *Trivia: a Journal of Ideas*, 7, 64–80.

Graves, R. (1961), *The White Goddess*, London: Faber & Faber.

Gray, Elizabeth Dodson (1982), *Patriarchy as a Conceptual Trap*, Wellesley, Mass.: Roundtable Press.

Groth, A. N. (1979), *Men Who Rape: The Psychology of the Offender*, New York: Plenum Press.

Harari, H. and Kaplan, R. M. (1977), *Psychology: Personal and Social Adjustment*, New York: Harper & Row.

Harding, Esther (1971), *Women's Mysteries*, London: Rider.

Hartley, Ruth (1959), 'Sex role pressures in the socialization of the male child', *Psychological Reports*, 5, reprinted in J. Pleck and J. Sawyer (eds) (1974), *Men and Masculinity*, Englewood Cliffs: Prentice-Hall.

Hegel, G. W. F. (1974 edn), *Lectures on the Philosophy of Religion* (3 vols), New York: Humanities Press.

Henderson, Joseph L. (1964), 'Ancient myths and modern man', in C. G. Jung (ed.), *Man and his Symbols*, London: Aldus Books.

Hillman, James (1978), *The Myth of Analysis*, New York: Harper & Row.

Hills, Virendra (1983), 'The courage to let go', *Soluna*, 4/4, 4–10 and 25–7.

Hite, Shere (1976), *The Hite Report on Female Sexuality*, London: Talmy Franklin.

Hite, Shere (1981), *The Hite Report on Male Sexuality*, London: Macdonald.

Hodson, Philip (1984), *Men . . .* , London: Ariel Books.

Horne, James R. (1978), *Beyond Mysticism*, Waterloo, Ontario: Wilfred Laurier University Press.

Jackins, Harvey (1965), *The Human Side of Human Beings*, Seattle: Rational Island.

James, E. O. (1963), *The Worship of the Sky God*, London: The Athlone Press.

James, Jenny (1985), *Male Sexuality: The Atlantis Position*, London: Caliban Books.

Janov, A. and Holden, M. (1977), *Primal Man: The New Consciousness*, London: Abacus.

Jourard, Sidney (1974), 'Some lethal aspects of the male role' in J. H. Pleck and J. Sawyer (eds), *Men and Masculinity*, Englewood Cliffs: Prentice-Hall.

Jung, Carl Gustav (1972), 'Introduction' in R. Wilhelm, *Secret of the Golden Flower*, London: Routledge & Kegan Paul.

Kaplan, S. R. (1978), *The Encyclopaedia of Tarot*, New York: U. S. Games Systems.

Kohlberg, Lawrence (1969), 'Stage and sequence: The cognitive-developmental approach to socialization', in D. Goslin (ed.), *Handbook of Socialization Theory and Research*, Chicago: Rand McNally.

Kokopeli, Bruce and Lakey, George (1982), 'Masculinity and violence', *Peace News*, 20 May 1977, reprinted in Pam McAllister (ed.), *Reweaving the Web of Life: Feminism and Nonviolence*, Philadelphia: New Society Publishers.

Korda, Michael (1972), *Male Chauvinism*, London: Coronet.

Kramarae, C. and Treichler, P. A. (1985), *A Feminist Dictionary*, Boston and London: Pandora Press.

Kramer, Samuel Noah (1969), *The Sacred Marriage Rite: Aspects of Faith, Myth and Ritual in Ancient Sumer*, Bloomington: Indiana University Press.

Lederer, Laura (ed.) (1980), *Take Back the Night; Women on Pornography*, New York: William Morrow.

Lindsay, Karen (1979), 'Compassion, altruism and man-hating', in E. and B. M. Shapiro (eds), *The Women Say: The Men Say*, New York: Dell.

Lingen, Gary (1983), 'Towards a new vision of manhood: Celebrating men's mysteries, positive male energy and the Horned One', *Brothers of the Earth Newsletter*, 1, 2–5.

Lingen, Gary (1985), 'Reconnecting our sexuality with our spirituality', *Brothersong*, 8, 5–7.

Loevinger, Jane (1976), *Ego Development*, San Francisco: Jossey-Bass.

Long, Pauline and Coghill, Mary (1977), *Is it Worthwhile Working in a Mixed Group?*, London: Beyond Patriarchy Publications.

Lorde, Audre (1981), 'The master's tools will never dismantle the master's house', in C. Moraga and G. Anzaldua (eds), *This Bridge Called my Back*, Watertown, Mass.: Persephone Press.

McAllister, Pam (ed.) (1982), *Reweaving the Web of Life: Feminism and Nonviolence*, Philadelphia: New Society Publishers.

McLean, A. (1983), *The Triple Goddess*, Edinburgh: Hermetic Research Series

Macy, Joanna Rogers (1983), *Despair and Personal Power in the Nuclear Age*, Philadelphia: New Society Publishers.

Mahrer, A. L. (1978), *Experiencing: A Humanistic Theory of Psychology and Psychiatry*, New York: Brunner/Mazel.

Maloney, George A. (1979), *Invaded by God: Mysticism and the Indwelling Trinity*, Denville, N. J.: Dimension Books.

Mann, Richard D. (1975), 'Winners, losers and the search for equality in groups', in Cary L. Cooper (ed.), *Theories in Group Processes*, London: John Wiley.

Marine, Gene (1972), *A Male Guide to Women's Liberation*, New York: Avon Books.

Maslow, A. H. (1968), *Toward a Psychology of Being*, New York: Van Nostrand Reinhold.

Matthews, C. and J. (1985), *The Western Way*, vol. 1, London: Routledge & Kegan Paul.

Miller, C. and Swift, K. (1979), *Words and Women: Language and the Sexes*, Harmondsworth: Penguin.

Miller, G. (1985), *The Double*, Oxford.

Miller, J. B. (ed.) (1973), *Psychoanalysis and Women*, Harmondsworth: Penguin.

Millett, Kate (1971), *Sexual Politics*, New York: Avon.

Morgan, Robin (ed.) (1970), *Sisterhood is Powerful*, New York: Vintage Books.

Negrin, Su (1972), *Begin at Start*, Washington: Times Change Press.

Nichols, S. (1980), *Jung and the Tarot: An Archetypal Journey*, York Beach: Samuel Weiser.

Oakley, Ann (1974), *Housewife*, London: Allen Lane.

Paton, K (1974), 'Crisis and renewal', *Self and Society*, vol. 2, no. 2, pp. 9–14.

Perera, Sylvia Brinton (1981), *Descent to the Goddess*, Toronto: Inner City Books.

Perry, John Weir (1966), *Lord of the Four Quarters: Myths of the Royal Father*, New York: George Brazillier.

Polyandron, Hermes (1985), 'Use of myth as a personal approach to deity and uncovering of the god element in it', *Brothersong*, 7, 6–9.

Red Therapy (1978), *Red Therapy*, London: Red Therapy.

Reynaud, Emmanuel (1983), *Holy Virility*, London: Pluto Press.

Rhodes, D. and McNeill, S. (eds) (1985), *Women against Violence against Women*, London: Onlywomen Press.

Rich, Adrienne (1978), *The Dream of a Common Language*, New York: Norton.

Riesman, David (1954), *The Lonely Crowd*, New York: Doubleday.

Robinson, Edward (ed.) (1978), *Living the Questions*, Oxford: RERU.

Rogers, Carl R. (1961), *On Becoming a Person*, London: Constable.

Rogers, Carl R. (1978), *On Personal Power*, London: Constable.

Rowan, John (1975), 'A growth episode', *Self and Society*, 3/11, 20–7.

Rowan, John (1976), *Ordinary Ecstasy: Humanistic Psychology in Action*, London: Routledge & Kegan Paul.

Rowan, John (1976a), *The Power of the Group*, London: Davis-Poynter.

Rowan, John (1979), 'Psychic celibacy in men', in O. Hartnett *et al.* (eds), *Sex-Role Stereotyping*, London: Tavistock Publications.

Rowan, John (1980), 'Patriarchy: What it is and why some men question it', *Self and Society*, 8/7, 207–12.

Rowan, John (1983), *The Reality Game: A Guide to Humanistic Counselling and Therapy*, London: Routledge & Kegan Paul.

Ruether, Rosemary Radford (1983), *Sexism and God-Talk: Toward a Feminist Theology*, Boston: Beacon Press.

Ryan, Tom (1985), 'Roots of masculinity', in A. Metcalf and M. Humphries (eds), *The Sexuality of Men*, London: Pluto Press.

Seidenberg, Robert (1973), 'Is anatomy destiny?', in J. B. Miller (ed.), *Psychoanalysis and Women*, Harmondsworth: Penguin.

Seidler, Vic (1985), 'Fear and intimacy', in A. Metcalf and M. Humphries (eds), *The Sexuality of Men*, London: Pluto Press.

Sexton, P. C. (1969), *The Feminized Male*, New York: Random House.

Shapiro, E. and B. M. (1979), *The Women Say: The Men Say*, New York: Dell.

Singer, June (1976), *Androgyny*, New York: Doubleday.

Sjöö, M. and Mor, B. (1981), *The Ancient Religion of the Great Cosmic Mother of All*, Trondheim: The Rainbow Press.

Snodgrass, Jon (ed.) (1977), *A Book of Readings for Men Against Sexism*, New York: Times Change Press.

Southgate, John and Randall, Rosemary (1978), *The Barefoot Psychoanalyst*, 2nd edn, London: AKHPC.

Spretnak, C. (ed.) (1982), *The Politics of Women's Spirituality: Essays on the Rise of Spiritual Power Within the Feminist Movement*, New York: Anchor.

Starhawk (1979), *The Spiral Dance: A Rebirth of the Ancient Religion of the Great Goddess*, San Francisco: Harper & Row.

Starhawk (1982), *Dreaming the Dark: Magic, Sex and Politics*, Boston: Beacon Press.

Steinem, Gloria (1984), *Outrageous Acts and Everyday Rebellions*, London: Fontana.

Stewart, R. J. (1985), *The UnderWorld Initiation*, Wellingborough: Aquarian Press.

Sullivan, C. *et al.* (1957), 'The development of interpersonal maturity', *Psychiatry*, 20.

Swain, Nina and Koen, Susan (1980), *A Handbook for Women on the Nuclear Mentality*, Norwich, Vt: Women Against Nuclear Destruction.

Swenson, Clifford (1973), *Introduction to Interpersonal Relationships*, Glenville, Ill.: Scott, Foresman.

Tapia, M. (1979), 'On machismo', in E. and B. M. Shapiro (eds), *The Women Say: The Men Say*, New York: Dell.

Underhill, Evelyn (1961), *Mysticism*, New York: E. P. Dutton.

Valiente, Doreen (1978), *Witchcraft for Tomorrow*, London: Robert Hale.

Valiente, Doreen (1984), *The ABC of Witchcraft*, London: Robert Hale.

von Eschenbach, W. (trans. A. T. Hatto) (1980), *Parzival*, Harmondsworth: Penguin.

von Franz, M-L. (1964), 'The process of individuation', in C. G. Jung (ed.) *Man and his Symbols*, London: Aldus Books.

Walker, Barbara (1983), *The Women's Encyclopaedia of Myths and Secrets*, San Francisco: Harper & Row.

Wallace, A. F. C. (1966), *Religion: An Anthropological View*, New York: Random House.

Warner, Marina (1978), *Alone of All Her Sex: The Myth and the Cult of the Virgin Mary*, London: Quartet.

Warnock, Donna (1982), 'Patriarchy is a killer: What people concerned about peace and justice should know', in Pam McAllister (ed.), *Reweaving the Web of Life: Feminism and Nonviolence*, Philadelphia: New Society Publishers.

Warren, Mary Anne (1980), *The Nature of Woman: An Encyclopaedia and Guide to the Literature*, Inverness, California: Edgepress.

Whitmont, Edward C. (1983), *Return of the Goddess*, London: Routledge & Kegan Paul.

Wilber, Ken (1980), *The Atman Project: A Transpersonal View of Human Development*, Wheaton: The Theosophical Publishing House.

Wilber, Ken (1981), *Up from Eden*, London: Routledge & Kegan Paul.

Wilber, Ken (1983), *Eye to Eye*, Garden City: Anchor Books.

Wolkstein, D. and Kramer, S. N. (1985), *Inanna, Queen of Heaven and Earth: Her Stories and Hymns*, Bloomington: Indiana University Press.

Woodcock, Bruce (1984), *Male Mythologies*, Brighton: Harvester Press.

Wright, Betsy (1982), 'Sunpower/Moonpower/Transformation', in Pam McAllister (ed.), *Reweaving the Web of Life: Feminism and Nonviolence*, Philadelphia: New Society Publishers.

# Index